Internet Marketing & SEO for Contractors

Everything you need to know to market your home services business online for More Calls, More Leads & Bigger Profits

By Josh Nelson & Dean Iodice

Joshua Nelson & Dean Iodice owners of ContractorSEO

Internet Marketing & SEO For Contractors

ISBN: 1492168726
ISBN-13: 978-1492168720

Warning and Disclaimer

www.ContractorSEO.net

DEDICATION

This book is dedicated to my beautiful wife, Yesenia Nelson, and my son Brandon. You are my inspiration and the reason I work so hard. In addition, my true passion in life is helping business owners increase their sales, grow their business and accomplish their goals. I want to thank all the wonderful contractors and home service professional that have allowed me to hone my craft by working with their business. You know who you are. I could not have written this book with out the real world experience that your company afforded me.

- Josh Nelson

CONTENTS

ACKNOWLEDGMENTS

We want to thank all the wonderful contractors and home service professional that have allowed me to hone my craft by working with their business. You know who you are. We could not have written this book with out the real world experience that your company afforded me.

We would also like to thank my current customers for who trusted in us to help build their businesses. Our team of great employees who work around the clock to get the job done at any cost. Building a great team is an important part of any business. Thanks Norton, Rolando, Alan, Jose T, Stephany, Luis and our great account managers who make our clients campaigns so successful, Jose L, Barbara and Chris. Without this great team none of what we have done and will do would ever be possible.

A special thank you to Charlie from QSC, you do everything you can to help us get the most out of our QSC membership. The entire PHCC and the local chapters that have had us out to speak. promote to and educate your members.

Thank you all

Josh and Dean
ContractorSEO

FREE BONUS
TRAINING VIDEO & GUIDE

As a buyer of this book you have access to a training video & implementation guide that go along with the material covered in this book. To access that training video just go to www.contractorseo.net/free

Go to www.contractorseo.net/free

1

YOUR ONLINE MARKETING PLAN
(WEBSITE, SEO, PPC, PAY-PER-LEAD SERVICES, ETC)

Congratulations on your purchase of "Internet Marketing & SEO for Contractors - Everything you need to know to market your home services business online for More Calls, More Leads & Bigger Profits," a complete overview of what it takes to maximize your opportunities online in terms of Leads, Calls and Revenue.

There are a number of channels/mediums to consider for your home service business when you look at the Online Marketing space. Whether you are a Roofer, AC Contractor, Pool Builder, Plumber, Landscaper, Painter, Electrician, Pest Control Company or some other home service-based business, this book has the plan for you.

At first glance, considering all of the marketing options available in your online marketing playbook might be overwhelming. Search Engines (Organic, Maps, Pay-Per-Click), Social Media (Facebook, Twitter, Google+, LinkedIn), Paid Online Directory Listings (Angie's List, YP.com, Yelp.com, etc.) and Paid Online Lead Services (Home Advisors, Networx, etc.). To maximize your lead flow from the internet, you need to develop a PLAN that covers each of these online marketing opportunities. The purpose of this book is to outline a plan with that will transform you from an online marketing novice to the dominant player in your area. Throughout this book, we will lay the foundation to map out your online marketing plan:

• Your online marketing plan (Website, SEO, PPC, Pay-Per-Lead services, etc.)
• Start with the fundamentals (Market, Message, Media) before jumping head first into your internet marketing strategy
• How to setup your website
• Understand how search engines work and learn the differences be tween the paid, organic and map listings
• **Search Engine Optimization** - How to optimize your website with key words that are most important for your particular business
     o How to conduct Keyword Research
     o Our list of the most commonly searched keywords broken down

by industry (Roofing, Landscaping, Kitchen Remodeling, Damage Restoration, Pest Control, Plumbing, HVAC, etc.)
- o How to achieve maximum result by mapping out the pages that should be included on your website
- o How to optimize your website for ranking in the organic listings on major Search Engines
- o How to improve your website's visibility so that you can rank on page one for your most important keywords
- o List of link building techniques and strategies that are proven to enhance rankings even in the post Penguin and Panda Era
- o Content marketing strategies for maintaining relevance in your market

- **Google Maps Optimization** - How to get ranked on the Google Map in your area
    - o The fundamentals of Google Maps ranking (NAP, Citations, Consistency and Reviews)
    - o How to establish a strong Name, Address, and Phone Number Profile
    - o How to properly claim and optimize your Google+ Local Listing and merge it with Google Places, if necessary
    - o How to merge your Google Places and Google+ Local listing if you have a preexisting Google Places account
    - o How to develop authority for your map listing via Citation De velopment
    - o List of the top citation sources for contractors and home service businesses
    - o How to get real reviews from your customers in your true service area
- Sample Review Card
- Sample Review Request Email
- Sample Review Us landing page for your website
- **Website Conversion Fundamentals** - How to ensure that your website converts visitors into leads in the form of calls and web submissions
- **Mobile Optimization** - How to optimize your website for mobile visitors
- **Social Media Marketing** - How to utilize Social Media (Facebook, Twit-

ter, Google+, LinkedIn and other social platforms for maximum effect in your contracting/home services business.

- **Video Marketing** - How to tap into the POWER of YouTube and other video sharing websites to enhance your visibility and drive better con version
- Leverage email marketing tools (Constant Contact, Mail Chimp, etc) to connect with your customers on a deeper level, receive more reviews, get more social media connections and ultimately get repeat and referral business.
- Overview of Paid Online Advertising opportunities
- Pay-Per-Click Marketing (Google AdWords and Bing Search) - How to maximize the profitability of your Pay-Per-Click Marketing efforts
    o Why PPC should be part of your overall online marketing strategy
    o Why most PPC campaigns fail
    o Understanding the Google AdWords Auction process
    o How to configure and manage your Pay-Per-Click campaign for maximum ROI
- **Paid Online Directories** - What paid online directories should you con sider advertising in (Angie's List, YP.com, Yelp.com, Judies Book, Mer chant Circle, etc.)
- **Pay-Per-Lead and Lead Services** - How to properly manage Pay-Per-lead services for maximum return and long term gains
    o Sample lead follow up email sequence
- **Track, Measure and Quantify** - How to track your online marketing plan to ensure that your investment is generating a strong return.

When it comes to internet marketing for your contracting or home service business, there are a number of avenues to explore. In this chapter, we will briefly touch on the various internet marketing channels that are available, and then go into more detail throughout the book. This chapter serves as your "Marketing Plan" and roadmap going forward.

ONLINE MARKETING CHANNELS

1. Search Engine Optimization (Organic Listings and Map Listings)
2. Search Engine Marketing/PPC on Google AdWords and Bing Search Network
3. Social Media Marketing (Facebook, Twitter, Google+, LinkedIn)
4. Video Marketing
5. Email Marketing
6. Paid Directory Marketing (Angie's List, City Search, Judy's Book, Yelp, etc.)
7. Paid Lead Services (Home Advisor, eLocal, Contractors.com, etc.)

SEARCH ENGINE OPTIMIZATION

Search Engine Optimization (SEO) is the process of increasing your company's visibility on major search engines (Google, Yahoo, Bing, etc.) in the organic, non-paid listings as consumers are searching for your products or services.

There are three very critical components of Search Engine Marketing.

The three components are:
- **Paid Listings** – The area along the top and side that advertisers can bid on and pay for in order to obtain decent placement in the search engines.
- **Organic Listings** – The area in the body of the Search Engine Results page.
- **Map Listings** – These are the listings that come up beneath the paid listings and above the organic listings in a number of searches.

Search Engine Optimization involves getting your website to show up in the Organic and Map Listings. These listings account for a majority of the search volume. As depicted in the illustration below, more than 78% of searchers click on the Organic (non-paid listings) rather than the paid listings.

When most people think "Internet Marketing," they think Search Engine Optimization. However, you will begin to see that SEO is only a small piece of the MUCH BIGGER "Internet Marketing" puzzle for contractors.

SEARCH ENGINE MARKETING / PPC
Now that we have discussed SEO, let's talk about Search Engine Marketing or PPC (Pay-Per-Click). Google, Yahoo and Bing all have paid

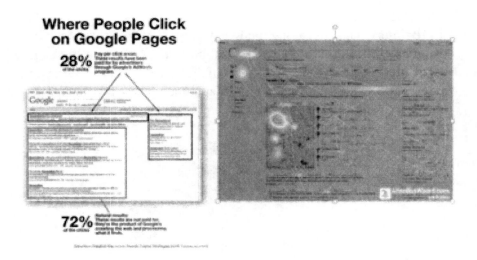

programs that allow you to BUY listings associated with your keywords to be placed in designated areas of their sites.

There are three really important benefits of PPC:
• Your keyword listings will appear on search engines almost immediately.
• You only have to pay when some actually clicks on your listing – hence the term Pay-Per-Click Marketing.
• You can get your ad to show up on national terms in the areas/cites in which you operate.

PPC Marketing works on an Auction system similar to that of eBay. You simply choose your keywords and propose a bid of what you would be willing to pay for each click. There are a number of factors that determine placement which will be discussed in detail in the PPC for Contractors chapter. But, in the broadest sense, the contractor who is willing to pay the most per click will be rewarded the top position in the search engines, while the second-most will be in the second position, etc.

PPC Marketing is a great way to get your company's website to appear at the top of the search engines right away, driving qualified traffic to your website.

SOCIAL MEDIA MARKETING

There is a lot of BUZZ around Social Media (Facebook, Twitter, Google+, LinkedIn, YouTube), but how can it be utilized by a Home Services Contractor? How can you use social media to grow your Contracting Business?

• More than 500 million active users
• 50% of our active users log-on to Facebook on any given day
• Average user has 130 connections
• People spend over 700 billion minutes per month on Facebook

So, how can you employ this amazing tool to grow your business? Use it to connect with your personal sphere of influence, past and new customers. By doing so, you can solidify and maintain existing relationships, remain Top-Of-Mind and ultimately Increase Repeat and Referral Business.

VIDEO MARKETING

Did you know that YouTube is the second-most used search engine on the market? Would you guess that it is ahead of Bing and Yahoo? It's true! Millions of people conduct YouTube searches on a daily basis. Most contractors are so focused on SEO that they completely neglect the opportunities that video and YouTube provide. By implementing a Video Marketing Strategy for your business, you can get additional placement in search results for your keywords, enhance the effectiveness of your SEO efforts and improve visitor conversion.

EMAIL MARKETING

Similar to Social Media Marketing, Email Marketing is a great way to remain top-of-mind with your customers and increase repeat business and referrals. Compared to direct mail and newsletters, email marketing is by far the most cost effective means to communicate with your customers. As we will discuss in the Email Marketing for Contractors chapter, we feel that email marketing can be used to effectively draw your customers into your social media world.

PAID DIRECTORY MARKETING

There are a number of Online Directories that are important for contractors:

1. Angie's List
2. YP.com
3. Judies Book
4. City Search
5. Merchant Circle
6. Yelp
7. Kudzu

PAID LEAD SERVICE SITES

There are an array of services that will sell you leads on a "pay-per-lead" basis or a flat monthly fee.

• Home Advisor
• eLocal Plumber, Roofer, Etc.
• Contractors.com

While these leads tend to go to a number of different providers and will be less qualified than other sources, these Pay-Per-Lead services can be a profitable online marketing channel if executed correctly.

Now that you have an understanding of each of the Internet Marketing Channels available, in the following chapters we will discuss how you can leverage them to connect with new customers and grow your contracting business.

WHERE TO START?

With such a large amount of internet marketing channels, where should you start? I firmly believe that over time, you should be appropriating each of these online marketing opportunities. However, you must first begin with the foundation - your website, organic rankings and social media/email. You should start looking at the various paid marketing opportunities when your website is setup correctly, ranking on search engines for your most important keywords in the organic, non-paid listings and you are actively engaging in social media activity. We have found that the biggest and most impactful opportunity is getting ranked organically (in the non-paid listings). You may then leverage the additional profits in paid marketing to further augment your growth. Once you are ranking well organically and things are firing on all cylinders, then you can start to run a well managed Pay-Per-Click Campaign and explore paid online directory listings on Angie's List, YP.com, etc.

Next, lets look at the fundamentals of your overall marketing strategy before pressing forward into full implementation.

For more details on setting up your internet marketing plan and a video walking you through these concepts go to:

www.contractorseo.net/marketing-plan

2

START WITH THE FUNDAMENTALS (MARKET, MESSAGE, MEDIA) BEFORE JUMPING HEAD FIRST INTO YOUR INTERNET MARKETING STATEGY

Before we delve into internet marketing, SEO and social media marketing, I want to be sure we have built a strong marketing foundation. As I talk with Home Service Contractors across the United States, I have come to the realization that the vast majority of you tend to skip straight past the fundamentals of your marketing strategy and dive head-first into tactics (Pay-per-click adverting, SEO, Social Media, etc.).

So, what do I mean when I say "Fundamentals"? All marketing has 3 core components:

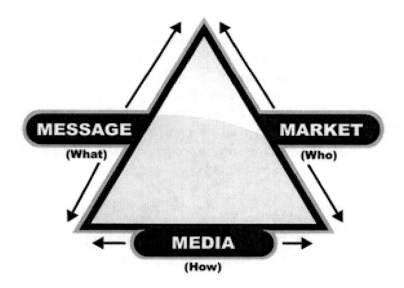

- Message (what)
- Market (who)
- Media (how)

You have to have a unique "Message" (who you are, what you do, what makes you unique, and why someone should hire you rather than another contractor), a specifically defined "Market" (who you sell to and who your BEST customers are), and THEN look at "Media" (where you can reach those BEST customers). The tactics (Pay-Per-Click, SEO, Social Media,

Direct Mail, etc.) fall into the "Media" category.

If you focus solely on the Media or Tactics, you will likely fail regardless of how well-selected that Media is. With that being said, you need to scale back to the fundamentals. You need to invest the time and energy in fleshing out your "Message" and figuring out who your "Market" is. By doing so, ALL of your Media choices will be vastly more effective. How can you do that?

Spend a few minutes and THINK. Take out a scratch pad and answer these questions:

MESSAGE

• What do I do that is unique and different from my competitors? (Do you offer a guaranteed time frame for your appointments? Do you offer writ ten estimates prior to starting work, promising to stand by that estimate? Maybe you offer a guarantee for all of your work and will repair any is sues within a one year period of time after the project is complete. May be you have recognized that people want to meet with a clean, profes sional and curious contractor, so your technicians are always dressed with crisp and clean collared shirts.)

• If you think about the psychology of a customer, what concerns or apprehensions do you think they have about hiring a contractor? ("They won't show up on time, so I will probably have to waste the whole day waiting around for them," or "they are going to be a crude mess and leave my place dirty," or "They are going to give me one price over the phone, tell me another when they get to the house and then charge me something VASTLY different once all is said and done."

• How can you address your customers' common concerns in a unique way.

MARKET

• Who is my ideal customer? (Please realize that not everyone resides in your city nor within a 25 mile radius of your office). You need to be more clear than that.

• Take a look at your last 25 customers and evaluate who spent the most money, who had the highest profit margins and who was genuinely pleased with your service. What are the unique characteristics of those good customers? Are they home owners vs. renters? Do they live in a particular area of town? Do they have a higher income level?

• Start to define who your ideal customer is so that you can put a market ing plan in place to attract similar customers.

Once you have fleshed out your Message and your Market you can start to think about Media. In order to determine what media will be most effective for you, you need to think about where you can reach your IDEAL customer.

Clearly, the internet is a great "media" for connecting with your ideal customer who is proactively in the market for your services. Throughout the remainder of this book, we will be explaining the various internet marketing channels and how you can use them to connect with your ideal customer.

Remember, you need to start with the FUNDAMENTALS (Message, Market and Media) before running headstrong into any marketing endeavor.

3

HOW TO SETUP YOUR WEBSITE

This chapter is all about how to setup your website. We are going to cover a lot of details as they relate to SEO, Google Maps Optimization, Pay-Per-Click Marketing, etc. However, without a properly designed and functioning website, those efforts will be put to waste. Before you can or even should begin exploring those options, you must have your website up and running.

Let's talk about website formats and the different options that are available to you when you are ready to start.

1. HTML Site – There are basic HTML pages and/or individual pages that can be incorporated into a website. This is how almost all websites were built several years ago. They had multiple pages hyper-linked together. HTML is still used today to build websites, one of the biggest disadvan tages is that when making changes or additions you must have knowl edge of the HTML markup language. If you are making changes to mul tiple pages it be very time consuming depending on how many pages you have on the site.

2. Template Based Site Builders - Site builders, that you can obtain through providers such as Go Daddy, and 1&1 are turnkey. You buy your domain and set up your website. I have found this type to be quite a bit less than ideal because you don't have a lot of control or flexibili-ty. But, there are still a lot of sites in this format. This is a propriatary system that does not give you any access to the back end of the site. This is bad because you have no control over the on page SEO that needs to be done to the site.

3. CMS Systems - Content Management Systems, like WordPress, Joom la, Drupal. I'm sure there are many others but these are the big ones.

As far as I'm concerned, a content management system is ideal for your business. The reason that I say that is because you have scalability. In any of these platforms, you have the ability to change your navigation on the fly, add as many pages as you need and easily scale out your site. If you have your website built in Website Tonight or in HTML format with graphics behind the website, and you wanted to add a new section, you would have to start from scratch. You would have to go back to the graphics and modify all of the pages in order to add the new section to your navigational structure. With a CMS, everything is built behind code allowing the ability to apply easy edits and to add multiple pages.

As you will see in the search engine optimization section of the book, you will have the ability to have a page for each one of your services and each city that you operate in. A CMS allows you to create your pages in a scalable format without having to mess around with the graphics or do anything that is difficult to control. Also, it is easy to access, modify, and update. Using formats like WordPress and Joomla, you may access the back-end administrative area at yourcompany.com/login. After entering your username and password, you will find that there is a very easy to edit system with pages and posts that function similarly to Microsoft Word. You can input text, import images and press "save," forcing all new edits to be updated on your live website. It is easier than it looks and is very search engine friendly.

Content Management Systems have intelligently structured linking between pages and content, making it extremely search engine friendly. We have found that this method tends to be better than regular HTML or Website Tonight options. In a lot of cases, a blog is going to be automatically bolted onto a CMS based website providing you with a section where you may feed updates. In the SEO chapter, we cover the importance of creating consistent updates and blogging regularly.

Another benefit of content management systems is that you are provided with a variety of plugins that you can choose to incorporate on your website. You can easily pull in your social media feeds, YouTube Videos and check-ins. You may also syndicate your website to automatically post any new updates to your social media profiles. You can add map integration where people can click to either get instructions or view a heat map from where your technicians are providing service. There are a surplus of features available within a CMS that you can't necessarily do with a non-CMS type option.

Whether you are looking to build a website from the ground up, if you are just getting started, or you feel like you simply need a redesign, I highly suggest that you do so in a content management system: ideally in Word-Press. WordPress is a fantastic platform and very easy to use. It's the most adopted website platform available with a lot of developers working on it. It's constantly being updated and improved and I have found it to work very well for contractors and Home Service type businesses.

You have my stamp of approval to go out and build your website on a WordPress platform.

WHAT SHOULD YOUR WEBSITE HAVE?

So, what should your website have? What navigation structure should you create? You definitely want to have:

1. Home
2. About Us
3. Our Services
4. Our Service Area (You will understand what I mean once you read the SEO Chapter)

5. Online Specials or Coupons
6. Reviews and Testimonials
7. Before and Afters or a Work Showcase
8. Buyers Guide
9. Blog
10. Contact Us

These are the core pages. Within "About Us," you might incorporate a drop down menu for subcategories including "Meet the Team," "Why Choose Our Company," etc. I think that's very powerful.

You want to be able to drive people back to a "Why Choose Us" section, and, in some cases, if you are having issues recruiting and retaining good quality talent, you might want to have a "Careers" page under the "About Us" navigation, where a visitor can go and fill out an application and learn more about your organization. Within "Our Services," you want to have the ability to list a drop down listing the types of services that you offer. We discuss this to a great extent in the SEO module. You want to have landing pages for each one of your services because they are going to be optimized with different keyword combinations. A "Service Area" section will give you the ability to show a heat map of all of the locations that your team goes, as well as a drop down menu that lists the sub-cities in which you operate within your market.

A "Reviews and Testimonials" page will provide you with a section to showcase what your customers are saying about you in text or video form. You can also pull in reviews from sites such as Google Maps, Angie's List, and Yelp. Finally, of cours, you will need a "Contact Us" page where web visitors have your general contact information.

These are the core things you should have on your website.

Outside of your navigational structure, what else should your website have? What other elements are going to help with conversion? Well, you should always provide a primary phone number on every page of your website, in the right hand corner. So, when somebody visits a page, their eyes are naturally drawn to the top section of the website, the logo and the phone number. People tend to expect that phone number will be somewhere in this location. It is ideal to have a prominent phone number, telling them to call you now for service in that section.

I believe that contractor websites should always make a web form available from which a customer can easily request a quote. Bear in mind that every visitor to your website is in a different situation and frame of mind. You may have someone that's on their phone or just leisurely looking to contact you for plumbing services and is able to simply pick up the phone and call you. On the other hand, somebody that's in a work environment may not have the ability to stop what they are doing and make a phone call without drawing attention from his or her coworkers. However, they may be able to browse around online to find out what options are available. Your potential customers reach your website and they are torn between making a call right at that moment, just scheduling the appointment, or wanting to have someone from your team contact them. Make it easy for them to enter their information into a web form where they can provide their name, phone number, email address, and a note detailing their requests that they can send through online. It makes it easier and doesn't create any pressure.

You also want to provide links to your social media profiles. Link to Facebook, Twitter, Google+ and LinkedIn so customers can easily jump off, engage with you on social media, see what you're doing and be able to press that important "like," "follow" or "subscribe" button. It helps create a sense of authenticity when your customers get to see your social media content.

Have a direct link that drives visitors to your online reviews and testimonials that we discussed previously. You should also post your credentials either in the sidebar or in the header graphic, proving, for example, that you're BBB-accredited or a member of the local chamber of commerce or industry association. This allows potential customers to rest assured that you are a credible organization, that you're involved in the community and that you're less apt to provide them with ill-service. They'll feel more comfortable doing business with you.

You definitely need to have your company name, address and phone number on every page of your website. It is not critical that you list your address on each page because it will not be a determining factor in whether or not they call you, but as I will explain in the Google Maps optimization chapter, having name, address and phone number consistency is critical for ranking on the Google Map.

It is a great strategy to have your name, address and phone number referenced on your website, ideally in the footer section. You need to have that contact information on all of your pages including the Contact Us page, of course.

It's extremely important that you infuse personality into your website. By personality, I'm referring to authentic photos and videos. Showcase your company, feature yourself, the business owner, and the people that work in the business; the technicians, the office team, etc. Showcase the office itself, the trucks and the equipment. Don't use stock photography, but authentic imagery. This gives the visitor the chance to get to know, like and trust you, before they even pick up the phone. I've seen this tactic prove itself time and time again.

Say a potential customer visited two different sites. One of them is generic; here's the same image he or she has seen before of the same plumbing guy with the wrench and the weird smile. The other website highlights a genuine picture of the owner, the team and equipment. This authentic page converts 10 to 1. You must let your real personality reflect on the website.

You must also craft messaging that explains why they should choose your company. Why should someone choose you over the competition? Pull them down a path where they can start to learn more about why you are they're best option. Where they can see your online reviews, and if they're kind of on the fence, where they can quickly locate some special offers and incentives that will drive action. That will get them to contact you right away, as opposed to continuing to browse the web for someone else.

The other major thing you want to think about, from the conversion perspective, is having a mobile-ready version of your website. More and more people are accessing the Internet via smart phones such as iPhones and Android phones. You need to make sure that the mobile version of your site isn't the same as your regular site. It should be condensed, fitting their screen and giving them just the information that they need. It should integrate with their phone so all they have to do is press a button to call you. People that are searching or accessing your website from a mobile device are in a different state of mind than the people that are browsing and finding you on a computer. Make it easy for them to get the information they need and to get in touch with you.

For more details on setting up your internet marketing plan and a video walking you through these concepts go to:

www.contractorseo.net/marketing-plan

4

UNDERSTANDING HOW SEARCH ENGINES WORK AND THE DIFFERENCES BETWEEN THE PAID, ORGANIC AND MAP LISTINGS

In this section, we wanted to take a few minutes to demystify the search engines and break down the anatomy of the Search Engine Results Page. By understanding how each component works, you can formulate a strategy to maximize your results.

There are three core components of the Search Engines Results page:

1. Paid/PPC Listings
2. Map Listings
3. Organic Listings

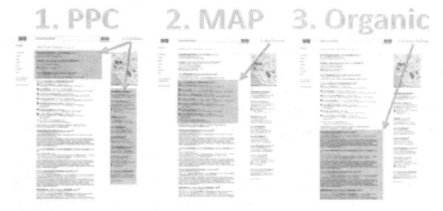

1. Paid/PPC Listings – In the paid section of the search engines you are able to select keywords that are relevant to your business, and then pay to be listed amongst the search results. The reason it is referred to as PPC or Pay-Per-Click is because rather than paying a flat monthly or daily fee for placement, you simply pay each time someone clicks on the link.

2. Map Listings – The map listings have become very important because they are the first things that comes up in search results for most locally based searches. If someone searches "AC Repair + your city," chances are the map listings will be the first thing they look at. Unlike the paid section of the search engine, you can't buy your way into the Map Listings. You have to earn it. Once you do, there is no per-click cost associated with being in this section of the search engine.

3. Organic Listings – The organic/natural section of the Search Engine Results page appears directly beneath the Map Listings in many local searches, but appears directly beneath the Paid Listings in the absence of the Map Listings (the Map Section only shows up in specific local searches). Similar to the Map Listings, you can't pay your way into this section of the search engines and there is no per-click cost associated with it. Now that you understand the three major components of the Search Engine Results and the differences between Paid Listings, Map Listings and Organic Listings you might wonder… "What section is the most important?" This is a question that we receive from plumbing contractors every day.

The fact is that all three components are important, and each should have a place in your online marketing program because you want to show up as often as possible when someone is searching for plumbing services in your area. With that said, assuming you are operating on a limited budget and need to make each marketing dollar count, you need to focus your investment on the sections that are going to drive the strongest Return On Investment.

Research indicates that the vast majority of the population looks directly at the Organic and Map Listings when conducting a search, and their eyes simply glance over the Paid Listings (as illustrated by the images below).

So, if you are operating on a limited budget and need to get the best bang for your buck, you should start by focusing your efforts on the area that gets the most clicks at the lowest cost. We have found that placement in the Organic and Map section on the Search Engines drive a SIGNIFIGANTLY higher Return On Investment than Pay-Per-Click Marketing. Begin with the Organic Listings and then, as you increase your profits, you can start to shift those dollars into a proactive Pay-Per-Click Marketing effort.

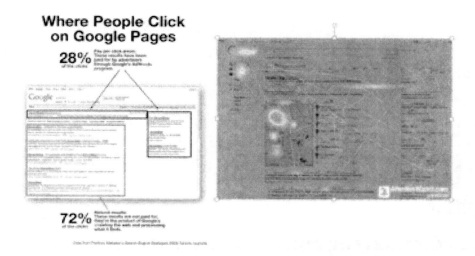

In the next chapter, we will start to look at Search Engine Optimization and how to optimize your website to rank in the organic listings (non-paid) for the most important keywords in your field.

5

SEARCH ENGINE OPTIMIZATION – HOW TO OPTIMIZE YOUR WEB-SITE FOR THE KEYWORDS THAT ARE MOST IMPORTANT FOR YOUR PARTICULAR BUSINESS

Getting your home services company listed in the organic section (non-paid-listings) of the Search Engines comes down to two core factors:

• Having the proper on-page optimization so that Google knows what you do and the general area that you serve. This allows it to put in the index for the right keywords. You do this by having pages for each of your services and then optimizing them for specific keyword combinations (Ex. Your City + main service, Your City + service 2, Your City + service 3, etc.).

• Creating enough authority and transparency so that Google ranks you on Page One (rather than page ten) for those specific keywords. Ultimately, it comes down to having credible inbound links and citations from other websites to your website and it's sub-pages. He who has the most credible inbound links, citations and reviews will be the most successful.

Throughout the course of this chapter I will provide specific how-to information on exactly what pages to add to your home services website and why. I will also discuss what you can do to improve your authority/transparency in Google's eyes so that your website ranks on Page One for the keywords that are most important to your business.

Before you start creating pages and trying to do the "on-page optimization" work, you need to be clear on the most commonly searched keywords relative to the services you offer. By understanding the keywords, you can be sure to optimize your website for the words that will actually drive qualified traffic to your site. Our team has done a great deal of due diligence and developed the following list of the most commonly searched keywords for the following services, listed at the end of this chapter: Plumbing, Roofing, HVAC, Landscaping, Pest Control, Kitchen Remodeling, and Pool Construction.

If you happen to be work in a different industry than what is listed and you wish to learn the methodology behind selecting these keywords, we have provided an overview of how to conduct keyword research.

How to conduct Keyword Research to determine what your customers are searching when they need your services.

There are a number of tools that can be used to conduct keyword research. Some are free of charge and others have a monthly cost associated with them. Some of the better keyword research tools include Wordstream,

Google Ad Planner and SEM Rush.

For the purposes of this book, we have developed instructions based on the free Google Ad Planner tool.

• Develop a list of your services and save it in a .txt file
• Develop a list of the cities that you operate in (your primary city of service and the smaller surrounding towns) and save it in a .txt file
• Go to www.mergewords.com
      o Paste your list of cities in column 1
      o Paste your list of services in column 2
      o Press the "Merge!" button
      o The tool will generate a list of all your services combined with your cities of service
• Go to Google.com and search "Google Keyword Tool" or go directly to https://adwords.google.com/o/KeywordTool
      o Paste your list of merged keywords into the "word or phrase" box
      o Press "Submit"
• You will now see a list of each of your keywords with a "search volume" number beside it
• Sort the list from greatest to smallest

You now have a list of the most commonly searched keywords in your area.

With this list you can map out keywords to specific pages on your website and rest assured that you are basing your strategy on opportunity rather than a guestimate.
For more details on how to conduct keyword research got online to www.contractorseo.net/keyword-research

Our list of the most commonly searched keywords broken down by industry (Plumbing, Landscaping, Kitchen Remodeling, Damage Restoration, Pest Control, Plumbing, and HVAC)

Below you will find the list of the most commonly searched keywords for Plumbing, Roofing and HVAC.

MOST SEARCH PLUMBING KEYWORDS:

KEYWORD	LOCAL MONTHLY SEARCH
plumbing	6,120,000
plumber	4,090,000
water heaters	1,830,000
bathroom remodeling	301,000
tankless water heaters	301,000
leak detection	201,000
drain cleaning	165,000
shower repair	90,500
boiler repair	90,500
plumbing contractor	49,500
emergency plumber	49,500
water heater repair	49,500
shower installation	49,500
water heater installation	40,500
sewer repair	22,200
commercial plumbing	18,100
commercial plumber	14,800
repipe	12,100
backflow testing	12,100
repiping	9,900
residential plumbing	8,100
tankless water heater installation	6,600
sump pump repair	5,400
residential plumber	5,400
garbage disposal installation	5,400
water softener installation	5,400
gas line installation	4,400
water softener repair	4,400
clogged toilet repair	3,600

sewer line replacement	3,600
hydro jetting	3,600
trenchless sewer repair	2,900
gas line repair	2,400
trenchless sewer replacement	2,400
slab leak repair	1,600
tankless water heater repair	1,600
burst pipe repair	1,000
septic tank plumbing	720
water filtration system installation	390

Based on this data, in order to get the most from the internet from a SEO perspective, you will want to create content on your website for the following keyword combinations:

Your City + plumbing
Your City + plumber
Your City + water heaters
Your City + bathroom remodeling
Your City + tankless water heaters
Your City + leak detection
Your City + drain cleaning
Your City + shower repair
Your City + boiler repair
Your City + plumbing contractor
Your City + emergency plumber
Your City + water heater repair
Your City + shower installation
Your City + water heater installation
Your City + sewer repair
Your City + commercial plumbing
Your City + commercial plumber
Your City + repipe
Your City + backflow testing
Your City + repiping

Your City + residential plumbing
Your City + tankless water heater installation
Your City + sump pump repair
Your City + residential plumber
Your City + garbage disposal installation
Your City + water softener installation
Your City + gas line installation
Your City + water softener repair
Your City + clogged toilet repair
Your City + sewer line replacement
Your City + hydro jetting
Your City + trenchless sewer repair
Your City + gas line repair
Your City + trenchless sewer replacement
Your City + slab leak repair
Your City + tankless water heater repair
Your City + burst pipe repair
Your City + septic tank plumbing
Your City + water filtration system installation

MOST COMMONLY SEARCH ROOFING KEYWORDS

KEYWORD	LOCAL MONTHLY SEARCH
roof	5,000,000.00
how to roof	5,000,000.00
roofing	2,740,000.00
roofs	450,000.00
metal roofing	246,000.00
roofing shingles	201,000.00
roof shingles	201,000.00
steel roofing	201,000.00
roofer	165,000.00
roofing contractor	165,000.00
roof repair	165,000.00
roofing contractors	165,000.00

roofing companies	165,000.00
roofers	165,000.00
shingle roof	135,000.00
how to shingle a roof	135,000.00
roofing company	135,000.00
new roof	90,500.00
roof replacement	74,000.00
roofing repair	74,000.00
roofing supplies	74,000.00
roofing materials	60,500.00
roofing material	60,500.00
roof materials	60,500.00
roofing cost	49,500.00
new roofing	49,500.00
roof installation	40,500.00
commercial roofing	40,500.00
roofing products	40,500.00
roofing installation	33,100.00
roof contractors	33,100.00
roof contractor	33,100.00
roofing costs	33,100.00
roofing prices	33,100.00
roofing systems	27,100.00
roof repairs	27,100.00
rubber roofing	27,100.00
roof leak	27,100.00
slate roof	22,200.00
roofing service	18,100.00
best roofing	18,100.00
residential roofing	18,100.00
roofing repairs	18,100.00
roofing calculator	14,800.00
types of roofing	14,800.00
roofing shingles prices	14,800.00
steel roofing prices	12,100.00

abc roofing	12,100.00
concrete roof	12,100.00
charlotte roofing	12,100.00
roofing services	9,900.00
flat roofs	9,900.00
epdm roofing	9,900.00
clay roof	9,900.00
re-roofing	8,100.00
re roofing	8,100.00
roofing tar	8,100.00
metal roofing installation	8,100.00
roof repair cost	8,100.00
roof repair contractors	8,100.00
roofing felt	8,100.00
leaky roof	8,100.00
roofing phoenix	8,100.00
copper roofing	8,100.00
roofing estimates	6,600.00
metal roof installation	6,600.00
flat roof repair	6,600.00
concrete tile roof	6,600.00

Based on this data, in order to get the most from the internet from a SEO perspective, you will want to create content on your website for the following keyword combinations:

Your City + Roofer
Your City + Roofing
Your City + Roofing Contractor
Your City + Roofing Service
Your City + Re Roof
Your City + Roof Repair
Your City + Roofers
Your City + Roofing contractors
Your City + Roofing Services

Your City + Commercial Roofer
Your City + Commercial Roofing Contractor
Roofer In Your City
Roofing In Your City
Roofing Contractor In Your City
Roofing Service In Your City
Reroof In Your City
Roof Repair In Your City
Roofers In Your City
Roofing contractors In Your City
Roofing Services In Your City
Best Roofer in Your City

MOST COMMONLY SEARCHED HVAC KEYWORDS

KEYWORD	LOCAL MONTHLY SEARCH
air conditioning	16,600,000.00
air conditioner	13,600,000.00
ac air conditioning	9,140,000.00
furnace	5,000,000.00
air conditioners	3,350,000.00
hvac	1,830,000.00
air condition	1,500,000.00
trane	1,220,000.00
air con	1,220,000.00
hvac air conditioning	1,000,000.00
heat pump	823,000.00
heating air	823,000.00
heating & air	823,000.00
heating and air	823,000.00
air conditioning units	823,000.00
air conditioning unit	823,000.00
air conditioner unit	673,000.00
air conditioner units	673,000.00
heating & cooling	673,000.00

cooling and heating	673,000.00
heating and cooling	673,000.00
air conditioning cooling	673,000.00
heat and air	550,000.00
air conditioning and heating	550,000.00
heating and air conditioning	550,000.00
heating air conditioning	550,000.00
heating & air conditioning	550,000.00
air conditioning heating	550,000.00
portable air conditioner	450,000.00
air conditioner portable	450,000.00
central air	368,000.00
portable air conditioning	368,000.00
air conditioning portable	368,000.00
portable air conditioners	368,000.00
air conditioners portable	368,000.00
air conditioning system	368,000.00
air conditioning repair	301,000.00
repair air conditioning	301,000.00
air conditioner price	301,000.00
window air conditioner	301,000.00
air conditioner repair	246,000.00
portable air conditioning units	246,000.00
repair air conditioner	246,000.00
air conditioning systems	246,000.00
air conditioner system	246,000.00
portable air conditioning unit	246,000.00
ac compressor	246,000.00
split air conditioner	246,000.00
duct cleaning	201,000.00
air conditioning price	201,000.00
ac unit	201,000.00
air conditioner prices	201,000.00
window air conditioning	201,000.00
window air conditioners	201,000.00

air conditioning service	201,000.00
service air conditioning	201,000.00
cost air conditioner	201,000.00
air conditioner cost	201,000.00
ac repair	165,000.00
cost of air conditioning	165,000.00
air conditioning cost	165,000.00
air conditioning compressor	165,000.00
air conditioning prices	165,000.00
heater repair	165,000.00
air conditioner systems	165,000.00
air conditioners price	165,000.00
air conditions	165,000.00
ac units	165,000.00
air conditioner service	165,000.00
service air conditioner	165,000.00
air conditioning equipment	165,000.00
split air conditioners	165,000.00
hvac heating	165,000.00

Based on this data, in order to get the most from the internet from a SEO perspective, you will want to create content on your website for the following keyword combinations:

Your City + air conditioning
Your City + air conditioner
Your City + ac air conditioning
Your City + furnace
Your City + air conditioners
Your City + hvac
Your City + air condition
Your City + trane
Your City + air con
Your City + hvac air conditioning
Your City + heat pump

Your City + heating air
Your City + heating & air
Your City + heating and air
Your City + air conditioning units
Your City + air conditioning unit
Your City + air conditioner unit
Your City + air conditioner units
Your City + heating & cooling
Your City + cooling and heating
Your City + heating and cooling
Your City + air conditioning cooling
Your City + heat and air
Your City + air conditioning and heating
Your City + heating and air conditioning
Your City + heating air conditioning
Your City + heating & air conditioning
Your City + air conditioning heating
Your City + portable air conditioner
Your City + air conditioner portable
Your City + central air
Your City + portable air conditioning
Your City + air conditioning portable
Your City + portable air conditioners
Your City + air conditioners portable
Your City + air conditioning system
Your City + air conditioning repair
Your City + repair air conditioning
Your City + air conditioner price
Your City + window air conditioner
Your City + air conditioner repair
Your City + portable air conditioning units
Your City + repair air conditioner
Your City + air conditioning systems
Your City + air conditioner system
Your City + portable air conditioning unit

Your City + ac compressor
Your City + split air conditioner
Your City + duct cleaning
Your City + air conditioning price
Your City + ac unit
Your City + air conditioner prices
Your City + window air conditioning
Your City + window air conditioners
Your City + air conditioning service
Your City + service air conditioning
Your City + cost air conditioner
Your City + air conditioner cost
Your City + ac repair
Your City + cost of air conditioning
Your City + air conditioning cost
Your City + air conditioning compressor
Your City + air conditioning prices
Your City + heater repair
Your City + air conditioner systems
Your City + air conditioners price
Your City + air conditions
Your City + ac units
Your City + air conditioner service
Your City + service air conditioner
Your City + air conditioning equipment
Your City + split air conditioners

For an updated list of these keywords broken down by industry visit
www.contractorseo.net/keywords

How to map out the pages on your website for maximum result

Now that you are set to determine the most commonly searched keywords
in your field, you can begin mapping out the pages that need to be added

to your website.

Keep in mind that each page on your website can only be optimized for 1-2 keyword combinations. If you came up with 25 keywords then you are going to need at least 12 – 15 landing pages.

You need to be sure you have each keyword mapped to a specific page on your site.

KEYWORD	MAPPED TO WHAT PAGE
Main Keyword	Home
Keyword 1	Services - Keyword 1
Keyword 2	Services - Keyword 2
Keyword 3	Services - Keyword 3
Keyword 4	Services - Keyword 4
Keyword 5	Services - Keyword 5

So, for example, a roofing company might come up with the following keywords:

Roofer, Roofing, Roofing Contractor, Roof Repair Commercial Roofing Contractor

KEYWORD	MAPPED TO WHAT PAGE
City Roofing	Home Page
City Roofing Contractor	Home Page
City Roof Repair	Roof Repair Page
City Commercial Roofing Contractor	Commercial Roof Repair
City 2 Roofing	City 2 Roofing Page
City 2 Roofing Contractor	City 2 Roofing Page
City 2 Roof Repair	City 2 Roof Repair Page

Now that you have mapped out the pages that need to be included on your website, you can start thinking about how to optimize each of those pages for the major search engines (Google, Yahoo and Bing).

How to optimize your website and pages for ranking in the organic listings on Search Engines

Step 1 - Build the website and obtain more placeholders on the major search engines.

A typical home services website is has only 5-6 pages (Home – About Us – Our Services – Coupons – Contact Us). That does not create a lot of indexation or placeholders on the major search engines. Most contractors provide a wide variety of services, as covered in the Keyword Research section of this chapter. By building out the website and creating separate pages that highlight each of these services that are offered (combined with city modifiers), the contractor can get listed on the search engines for each of those different keyword combinations.

Here is an example:
• Home – About – Coupons – Contact Us
• Sub-pages for each service – Miami Emergency Plumber, Miami Leak Detection, Miami Toilet Repair, Miami Water Heater Installation, Miami Tankless Water Heater, ETC

They often provide services in a large number of locations outside of their primary city. In order to be found on the major search engines for EACH of those sub-cities, additional pages need to be created:

• Sub-pages for each sub-city serviced – Kendall Plumber, Doral Plumber, Homestead, Plumber, etc.

Step 2 - Optimize Pages for Search Engines:
Once the pages and sub-pages are built for each of your core services, each page need to be optimized from an SEO perspective in order to make the search engines understand what the page is about. Here are some of the most important items that need to be taken care of for on-page search engine optimization:

- Unique Title Tag on each page
- H1 Tag restating that Title Tag on each page
- Images named with primary keywords
- URL containing page keyword
- Anchor Text on each page and built into Footer – Miami Plumber
- XML Sitemap should be created and submitted to Google Webmaster Tools and Bing Webmaster Tools

Optimized Title Tag

Typical Plumbing Site Title

- Joe's Plumbing

SEO Optimized Title Tag

- Orlando Plumber | Shamrock Plumbing Orlando, Fl | Orlando Repipe

Optimized Title Tag

SEO Optimized Title Tag

- Orlando Emergency Plumbing - 24 Hour Emergency Plumbing Service in Orlando, FL
- Orlando Water Heater Repair - Water Heater Repair Service in Orlando, Fl
- Orlando Drain Cleaning - Drain Cleaning Service in Orlando, Fl Etc

How to build up the authority of your website so you can rank on page one for your most important keywords

Once the pages are built and the "on-page" SEO is complete, the next step is getting inbound links. Everything we have discussed to this point is sort of like laying the ground work –the pages need to be in order to even be in the running. However, it is the number of QUALITY inbound links and web references to those pages that is going to determine placement.

30% of SEO is On-Page type work
The other 70% is Link Building

Once the pages are built is just the beginning. The only way to get your site to rank above your competition is by having MORE quality inbound links and citations to your site.

He Who Has The MOST Quality Inbound Links WINS!

Again, if there is any secret sauce to ranking well in the search engines, it really is links and authority. The major caveat to that is that you can't just use garbage links. You don't want to just have a thousand links. When I say links, I'm referring to other websites hyper linking to your website, which I'll explain a little bit more with specific examples.
The latest algorithm changes (Google Panda and Google Penguin) involve Google trying to prevent spam. A lot of internet marketers and SEO coordinators realize it's all about the links. That is what the Google algorithm was built upon. They figured out ways to get a variety of links with random anchor text pointed back to the pages that they want to have ranked. Google has recognized that if those links are not relevant then they don't add any value to the internet.

Bad or irrelevant links can actually hurt your ranking more than help it. It's about getting quality, relevant links back to your home page and sub pages through content creation and strategic link-building. How do you get the links? Where do you get the links? Take a look at the visual below as a point of reference. I call this my circle of linking opportunities:

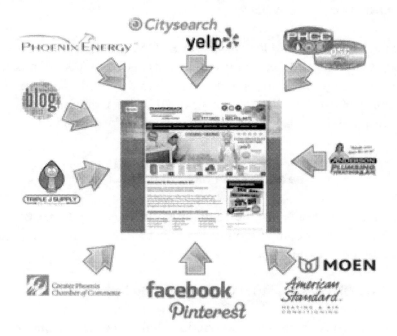

1. Association Links – Be sure that you have a link to your site from any industry associations that you belong to (Ex. Plumbing association, Chamber of Commerce, Networking Groups, etc.).

2. Directory Listings – Get your site listed on as many directory type websites as possible (Angie's List, Yahoo Local Directory, Judy's Book, Yelp. com, etc.)

3. Create Interesting Content/Articles about your industry - This is probably the #1 source of inbound links. For example, you can write an article about "hot water heaters" and push it out to thousands of people through article directory sites that may each contain a link back to a specific page on your site.

4. Competitive Link Acquisition – this is the process of using tools like Raven Tools, SEO Book and others to see what links your top competitors have, and then get those same or similar links pointed back to your website.

DIRECTORY LINKS

There's a number of what I like to call "low hanging fruit" links. It all starts with your online directory listings. Some examples include Google Maps, Yahoo Local, City Search, Yelp.com, Judy's Book, Best of the Web, Yellow Pages, Hot Frog, eLocal Plumber, Service Magic, and the list goes on. All of those online listings let you list your company name, address, phone number and a link back to your website. Some of them even allow reviews.

For the most part, adding your business information to those directories is completely free of charge. You want to make sure that you have your company listed on as many of the online directory listings as possible for authoritative linking reasons.

They're also valuable from the Google Maps optimization perspective because they give you citations, which are very important for getting ranked on the map. A great way to find additional online directories to add your company to would be to run a search in Google for "Your Company Type – Business Directory" or "Your City – Business Directory". This will give you a great list of potential directory sites to add your company to. There are also tools for this like BrightLocal or White Spark, that can provide you with a list of directory sources based on your industry. After beginning with online directory listings, you want to look at any associations that you're involved with.

ASSOCIATION LINKS

In the visual, I reference PHCC and QSC. I'm assuming you are involved in some type of association, whether it is the national industry association, the local chapter or some other group affiliation. Visit the websites of those organizations and get listed in the member section. This will give you citations and the opportunity to link back to your website.
Affiliated Industries and Local Businesses that are non-competitive - You can work with colleagues that have affiliated industry type businesses. If you're in plumbing, go to the HVAC contractors in your area and ask

if they will post a link to your website on their own site and vice versa. Utilizing your resources and teaming up with relevant companies will add more authority to your domain.

SUPPLIER SITES
The next thing you could look at is the suppliers that you purchase from. If you are a regular customer at American Standard, Moen or if you've got a co op agreement with Bryant or some other manufacturer, try to coordinate a deal with them. Oftentimes, the places where you buy your merchandise will have a section on their website that mentions their value add resellers. You can get a link from those.

SOCIAL MEDIA PROFILE LINKS
The other "low hanging fruit" links are social media profiles. We have a whole chapter about the power of social media and how you can harness it to get repeat and referral business. Simply from a link building perspective, you should set up a Facebook page, Twitter account, LinkedIn profile, Google Plus page, Pinterest profile and a You Tube channel and place a link to your website on each. Each one of them will allow you to enter your company's name, address, phone number a description and, of course, a place to put your website address.

LOCAL ASSOCIATION
Other local associations that you're involved in. If you're a member of the Chamber of Commerce, a networking group like BNI (Business Networking International), or if you're involved with a local charity, find out if they list their members on their websites. Another great place to get links is by typing in your city directory.

COMPETITIVE LINK ACQUISITION
You might be surprised that if you really tackle these elements and you don't do any of the other things we have discussed, you will notice that you've probably got enough links to outrank your competition in your area. I want to share some additional thoughts and strategies on how you

can accomplish even more from a link building perspective. A very powerful strategy that you can implement is called Competitive Link Acquisition.

The way I like to think of it is that if quantity inbound links are the secret sauce to outranking your competition, and if we could figure out who's linking to your competition or what links your competition have, and we can get those same or similar links pointed back to your website, then you can outrank them, because you'll at that point have more authority. Competitive link acquisition is the process of figuring out who is in the top position for your most important keywords, reverse engineering their link profile to see what links they have, and getting those same or similar links pointed back to your website. A simple way to do this is just to go to Google.com and type in "your city + your service," and find out who is in the top few positions. Let's take a look at the number one placeholder. He's there because his website is optimized well and Google knows that he should be ranked well based on the quality and quantity inbound links compared to the competition.

Once you know who he is, you can use a couple of different tools such as Raven Tools, Majestic SEO, Back Link Watch, etc., and you can take their URL, input it into your tool of choice, run the report, and get a list of links in return.

So, your number one competitor is competitor.com. Google spits out a list showing that they have 392 inbound links.

- He's got a link from the local Chamber of Commerce.
- He's got a link from the PHCC.
- He's got a link from an article that he posted in the local newspaper.
- He's got a link from the local networking chapter.

By analyzing the types of links that he has, you can systematically mimic those links and get them pointed back to your website.

Don't just do this for your first competitor, but also for your second and third and fourth and fifth competitors. By doing that on a consistent basis, you can start to dominate the search engines for your most important keywords.

If you build out your site for your services and sub-services, optimize the pages using SEO best practices and then systematically obtain inbound links,you will start to DOMINATE the search engines for the plumbing related keywords in your area.

Content marketing strategies for maintaining relevance in your market
Another highly important factor in SEO is relevant ongoing updates to your website. In the internet age, content is king.

Google loves fresh content. In some cases, with the changes in the algorithm, just because you've got a great website with the right title tags and all the best links, you may get discounted if they're not seeing fresh information posted on a consistent basis. It is important to have a methodology where you are creating and posting content to your website on a regular basis. I want to give you a framework for figuring out what kind of content you could write, why you should create content, and how you can do it consistently.

First, you need to understand and accept that you need to become a subject matter expert. You might not consider yourself a writer or a content creator, but you are a subject matter expert.

There are things that you know that the general population does not. You're a plumber, a roofer, a pool builder and you have a team of people that are experts in this area as well. You can create content on the topic that you know most about.

You can write about the differences between tank and tankless water heaters, why you would want to consider trenchless versus a regular project, or the differences between copper and PCB piping. There are a lot of different topics you can come up with that you can create content about.

You should also consider that content doesn't have to be just written words. It's doesn't have to be just articles. Content can come in a variety of forms. The most popular are going to be articles, photos, videos and audio files. Stop and think about what content creation method works best for you.

Some people are great writers and that's their strength. Other people like to be on camera. I personally like to create videos. I'm very comfortable creating videos.

Other people can talk, and they can talk your ear off about whatever topic they are passionate about. You can create content in many different ways. Because it is what I enjoy, I'll use video as an example. A contractor can set up a camera and record himself explaining the differences between using a tank and going tankless in the same manner that he would explain it to a customer.

Now you'll actually have multiple pieces of content. You'll have a video, which can be uploaded to You Tube, Vimeo, Meta Café, etc. That one piece of content can create multiple invaluable links to your website. You can also take that video, save the audio portion of it, and you've got an audio clip. You can upload that audio file to your website and post on other various sites. You can use a transcription service like Castingwords.

com, for instance, where you upload the audio or video file and somebody converts it to text. For a couple of bucks, you'll have a complete article comprised of what you said. Now you've got a piece of content you can post to your blog. You can put it on eHow or one of those other article directory sites.

You want to create content on a consistent basis, using the blog on your website as the hub to post it, but then syndicating it to various sources. Syndicating it to article directory sites if it's in text form, and sending it to video sites like Vimeo, Metacafe and YouTube.com if it's in video form. Doing this keeps the content fresh on your website/domain and creates a lot of authority, which is really going to help with the overall ranking of the website on the search engines.

You want to make sure you're appropriating each one of these link-building opportunities to maximize your rank-potential in your area. You might be surprised that contracting and home services are highly competitive from a SEO perspective. There are a lot of contractors that want to rank for the same keywords, and many of them have invested heavily in the internet and in getting themselves higher in the search engines.
Now that you've built out your website, you've optimized it correctly, and you've got an ongoing link-building and content development strategy in place, you want to start looking at Google Maps Optimization and getting ranked on the Google Map.

For more details on setting up your internet marketing plan and a video walking you through these concepts go to:

www.contractorseo.net/marketing-plan

6

GOOGLE MAPS OPTIMIZATION - HOW TO GET RANKED ON THE GOOGLE MAP IN YOUR AREA

The fundamentals of Google Maps ranking (NAP, Citations, Consistency and Reviews)

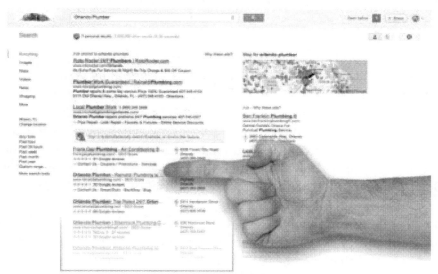

Getting listed on the first page of the Google Map for "Your City + Service" comes down to four primary factors:
• Having a claimed and verified Google Map Listing
• Having an optimized Google+ Local (Formerly Places) listing for the area that you operate in
• Having a consistent N.A.P. (Name, Address, Phone Number Profile) across the web so that Google feels confident that you are a legitimate organization located in the place you have listed and serving the market you claim to serve.
• Having reviews from your customers in your service area
  If you have each of these four factors working in your favor you will SIGNIFICANTLY improve the probability of ranking on page one of Google Maps in your market.

How to establish a strong Name, Address, Phone Number Profile

As I mentioned above, having a consistent Name, Address, Phone Number Profile across the web is essential for ranking well on the Google Map in your area. Google sees it as a signal of authority.

Rather than jumping directly into claiming your Google Map listing and citation-building, it's critical that you start by determining your true N.A.P. so that you can ensure that it is referenced consistently across the web.

When I say making sure that it's consistent, you want to be certain that you are always referencing the legitimate name for your business. If your company's name is "Bob's Plumbing Company", you must always list it as "Bob's Plumbing Company," as opposed to just "Bob's Plumbing."

The other thing you should be aware of is that there is a lot of misinformation about how to list your company name online. You may read information suggesting that you keyword your name. For example, if your name is "Bob's Plumbing," somebody might tell you it would be really smart if you just added to the title of your company "Bob's Plumbing | Dallas Plumber," for instance. While that may have worked back in the day, it's no longer an effective strategy. It's actually a violation of Google Places' policies and procedures. Make sure you list your exact company name the same way across the board on all of your directory sources. Also make sure that you use the same phone number in all of those places. I'm a big advocate for tracking phone numbers and what is happening with your marketing. But, when it comes to your online directory listings, you want to use your primary business phone number that you've been using from the beginning.

Don't try to create some unique number for each one of your directories. What that does is confuses your name/address profile. It will hurt you. Use your primary phone number in all of those places, use your exact company name, and use your principal address, written the same way. If your business is located at "1367 South West 87th Street, Suite Number 105," make sure you list it just like that every single time. Don't neglect to include the suite in one place and then put it on in another. Don't spell West" in one place and put "SW" in the other. We are driving fc consistent name/address profile across the web.

A good way to figure out what Google considers to be your N.A.P. is to run a search on Google for "Your Company" and see what is being referenced on the Google Map. See how that compares to the other high authority sites like YP.com, Yelp.com, Angie's List and others. Look for the predominant combination of N.A.P. and reference that for all your directory work going forward.

How to properly claim optimize your Google+ Local Listing and merge with Google Places if necessary.

Below you will find a step-by-step guide for checking, claiming and managing your Local Business Listings on Google.

1. Go to http://www.Google.com/places

2. Click on "I agree to the Terms of Service", then click the Okay button

3. Type your company name in the search box

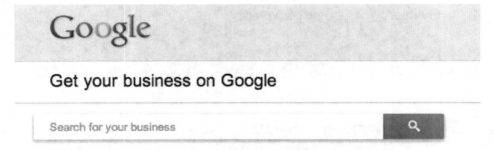

4. At this point in the process Google Places searches it's database for your business name. The next screen will display the results, keep in mind that the results will show every business in the country with the same business name. Be careful to select your exact business. If by chance you do not see your business listed the last selection on the screen will say "No, these are not my business".

The next few steps will show the steps to take if your business is listed and the process and if you are adding your business for the first time because it it not in Google's index.

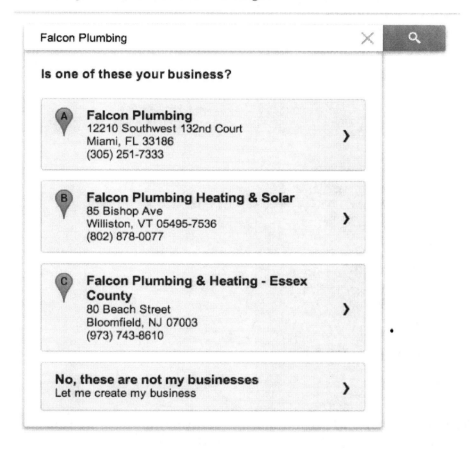

Google

Get your business on Google

Falcon Plumbing

Is one of these your business?

> (A) **Falcon Plumbing**
> 12210 Southwest 132nd Court
> Miami, FL 33186
> (305) 251-7333

> (B) **Falcon Plumbing Heating & Solar**
> 85 Bishop Ave
> Williston, VT 05495-7536
> (802) 878-0077

> (C) **Falcon Plumbing & Heating - Essex County**
> 80 Beach Street
> Bloomfield, NJ 07003
> (973) 743-8610

> **No, these are not my businesses**
> Let me create my business

5. If you see your business listed as indicated in the screen shot above, then select it and follow the next few steps.

6. Let's assume your business is the first one, simply click it, you will then be taken to the next screen which is the verification process.

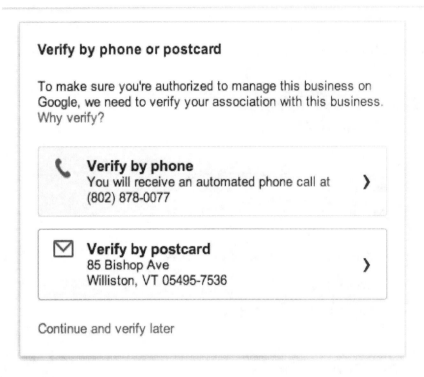

Google

Verify Falcon Plumbing Heating & Solar

Verify by phone or postcard

To make sure you're authorized to manage this business on Google, we need to verify your association with this business. Why verify?

☏ **Verify by phone**
You will receive an automated phone call at ⟩
(802) 878-0077

✉ **Verify by postcard**
85 Bishop Ave ⟩
Williston, VT 05495-7536

Continue and verify later

7. In some cases you have the option to verify by phone but we have seen that on rare occations, for the most part verification is via postcard. The postcard is mailed to your business in about 2 weeks with a pin number you need to enter into your Google Places listing.

The postcard system is a way for Google to control people claiming false listings. Although this seems like a pain it is a good quality measure to prevent some people from trying to falsify their business listing.

8. This final screen is for postcard verification and shows you what the poscard looks like so you and you team can be on the look out for it.

Verify Falcon Plumbing Heating & Solar

Verify by postcard

In one to two weeks, you'll get a postcard like this in the mail, which contains your PIN.

Google
Google Headquarters
1600 Amphitheatre Pkwy
Mountain View CA 94043

Falcon Plumbing Heating & Solar
85 Bishop Ave
Williston, VT 05495-7536
United States

Optional contact name

Send postcard   Cancel

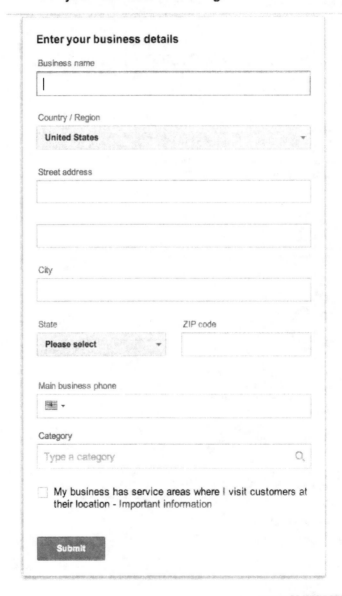

9. The next screen in the Google Places sign up process is to collect all your companys infoFill in all of the necessary information:

• Update Your Company Name to Read "Company Name") – E.G. Ad vance Plumbing. Don't add any additional keywords here.
• Select your region
• Add your street address, City, State and Zip Code.
  It's important to take note on how you enter this information for it will be your NAP across all the online directories.
• Catagory selection is another very important selection. Look through all the options and choose the one that best describes your business. For expample if you are a plumbing contractor, drill down deeper than just the contractor category.
• The last selection on the form as seen on the last page is a check box se lection, if you have a physical commercial office, yet customers DO NOT come to your place of business you must select this. You have to hide your address. The reason we point this out is because as you do searches you will indeed see businesses listed on the map that show their address and they are companys that customers do not visit. Don't take the attitude that if they can do it so can I. Start off right, in time Google will catch up with businesses not following their guidlines and remove them from Google Places. Trust me when I say it hurts so much more when you are there and removed than never being there at all.

10. Click Submit

11. Next you will be asked to confirm you listing via post card or tele-phone. If you get the option of doing it via telephone it is a much faster process. In the event that you do not get the telephone option then select the postcard option.

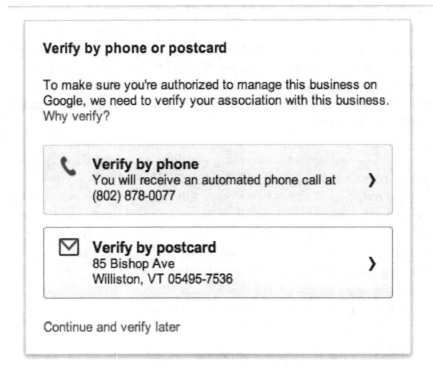

Google

Verify Falcon Plumbing Heating & Solar

Verify by phone or postcard

To make sure you're authorized to manage this business on Google, we need to verify your association with this business. Why verify?

Verify by phone
You will receive an automated phone call at
(802) 878-0077

Verify by postcard
85 Bishop Ave
Williston, VT 05495-7536

Continue and verify later

12. Upon selecting the postcard option you will see the following screen. It takes about 2 weeks to receive the postcard via the mail.

13. The screen shot on the text page is the next screen you will see showing an image of what the postcard looks like. Be on the lookout for it, they are hard to spot and look like marketing materials.

Google

Verify Falcon Plumbing Heating & Solar

Verify by postcard

In one to two weeks, you'll get a postcard like this in the mail, which contains your PIN.

Google

Google Headquarters
1600 Amphitheatre Pkwy
Mountain View CA 94043

Falcon Plumbing Heating & Solar
85 Bishop Ave
Williston, VT 05495-7536
United States

Optional contact name

Send postcard   Cancel

That's it! You have completed the 11 steps to claiming and setting up your Google Map listing on Google Places.

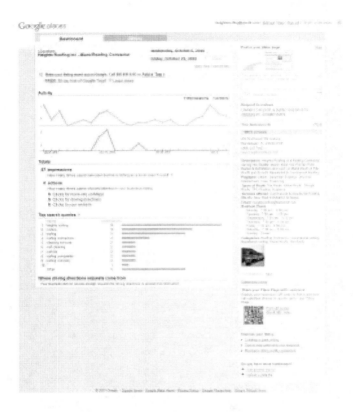

Here, you will be able to edit your listing, add a coupon and check our your Google Places page stats:

• How many people are pulling up your Google Places page
• What keywords are they searching to get to you
• How many of them are clicking on your site, etc.

Here is what you Google Map Listing will look like on Google once you are finished:

- Look for the "Business Owner Verified" check box in the top right corner.

THERE ARE A NUMBER OF BEST PRACTICES THAT YOU WANT TO BE AWARE OF TO PROPERLY OPTIMIZE YOUR MAP LISTING.

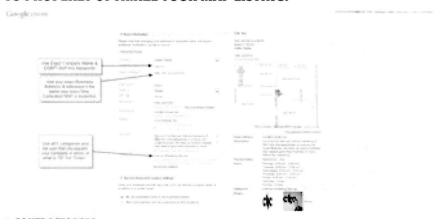

- **Company Name** – Always use your legal Company Name – don't cram additional words into the name field. Ex. If your company name is "Joe's Plumbing," don't try to put additional keywords like "Joe's Plumbing – Dallas". This would be against the Google Places guidelines and will reduce your probability of ranking.

- **Address** – On the "Address Field" use your EXACT legal address. You want to ensure that you have the same address listed on your Google Places listing as it is on all the other online directory listings like Yel lowPages.com, CitySearch.com, Yelp.com, etc. The consistency of your N.A.P. (Name, Address, Phone Number Profile) is very important for placement.

- **Phone Number** – Use a local number (not an 800 number), and make sure it is your real office number rather than a tracking number. We find that 800 numbers don't rank well. If you use a tracking number it won't be consistent with your other online directory listings and will result in poor ranking.

- **Categories** – You can use up to five categories, so use ALL five. Be sure to use categories that describe what your business "is" rather than what it "does". So you can use "Plumber" "Plumbing Contractor" and "Water Heater Repair Contractor," rather than "Plumbing Repair" or "Drain Cleaning." The latter would be considered a violation of Google's regulations and would hurt rather than help you.

- **Service Area and location settings** – Google offers two options here
1. No, all customers come to my location
2. Yes, I serve customers at their location.

As a home services business (Plumbing, HVAC, Roofing, etc.) you need to select "Yes, I serve.." because clearly you and your technicians are visiting the customers at their location. Not doing so can result in a penalty on your listing.

- The next option is "Do not show my address". If you work from a home office ,it is required that you select "Do not show my address." Not doing so puts you at risk of having your listing deleted.
- If you don't have a business address or a home address to list, the only other option is a Virtual Office. Unfortunately P.O. Box addresses and mail boxes don't tend to rank well.

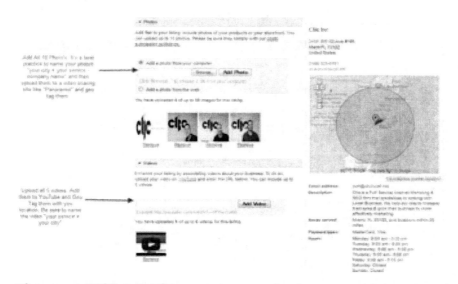

- **Picture and Video Settings** – You can upload up to ten pictures and five videos. Use this opportunity to upload authentic content about your company. It's always best to use real photos of your team, office, and equipment rather than stock photos.
- **Pictures** – You can get more juice from this section by saving the images to your hard drive with a naming convention like "your city + plumber – your company name," rather than the standard file name. You can also create geo context for the photos by uploading them to a video sharing site like Panoramio.com (a Google Property) that enables you to Geo

Tag your photos to your company's location.

• **Videos** – Upload VIDEOS. They don't have to be professionally pro duced and will resonate well with your customers. A best practice is to upload the videos to YouTube and then Geo Tag them using the advanced settings.

Once you have Optimized your listing using the best practices referenced above, you want to be sure that you don't have any duplicate listings on Google Maps. We have found that even just one or two duplicates can pre-vent your listing from ranking on page one. In order to identify and merge duplicate listings, run a search on Google for "Company Name, City".

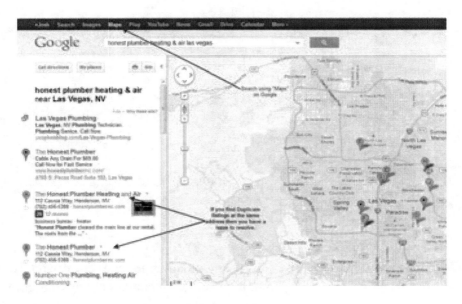

To clean up duplicates, click on the listing in question and then click "edit business details."

• Click "This is a duplicate" to let Google know that the listing should be merged with your primary listing.

If you follow these best practices you will have a well optimized Google Maps listing for your Plumbing Business. The next step is merge your Google Places Listing with Google+ Local.

For a video walk through of exactly how to properly claim your Google Map listing go to www.contractorseo.net/claim

HOW TO MERGE YOUR GOOGLE PLACES AND GOOGLE+ LOCAL LISTING IF YOU HAVE AN EXISTING GOOGLE PLACES ACCOUNT

Setup a personal Google Plus Profile (If you already have one, just login and skip to step 2).

STEP 1 – Login to your Google account (ideally the one tied to your Google Places Listing)
- You can tell if it is the right account by going to www.google.com/places
- If it shows you a dashboard with data you are in the right place
- To setup the personal Google+ Profile go to www.google.com/plus

STEP 2 – Setup Google+ Local PAGE

- In Google+ Personal Account click "More…" on the sidebar on the left and click "Pages"

- Create a new page by clicking "pages"
- Select "Local Business"

• Type in Phone Number (It should find your existing business)

• Click on "Your business listing"
• "Confirm your Info"
• List your external website
• Agree to terms and press OK
• Update categories, phone and profile picture and click "Finish"
• Update the business information

URGENT – Click "Unverified" or "In Progress"

• From there you can request the PIN Code and/or enter the PIN once you receive it in the mail

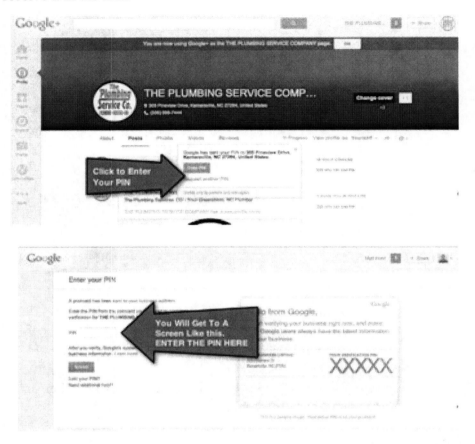

That's it. Once you enter the PIN, your listing will be verified and your Google+ Local Page will be merged with your Google Places listing!

The next step is to build the authority for your location through proactive citation development.

How to develop authority for your map listing via Citation Development

Now that you have claimed your Google Places Listing and optimized it to its fullest, you need to build authority. Having a well-claimed and optimized Google+ Local listing doesn't automatically rank you on page one. Google wants to list the most legitimate and qualified providers first. So, how do they figure out who gets the page one listings? Well, there are a number of determining factors, but one of them is how widely the company is referenced on various online directory sites such as Yellow Pages, City Search, Yelp and others.

Citations are web references to your company name, address and phone number. You can add citations in a variety of ways. There are directory listings that you should claim manually and others that you can submit to via submission services like Universal Business Listing or Yext.com. My personal preference is to claim listings manually, ensuring that I am in control and can make updates/edits as needed.

TOP CITATION SOURCES TO CLAIM MANUALLY:

• Google+ Local
• Bing Local
• Yahoo Local
• City Search
• Angie's List
• Yelp
• YP.com
• Merchant Circle
• Manta

LIST OF THE TOP CITATION SOURCES FOR CONTRACTORS AND HOME SERVICE BUSINESSES

Google
Google is probably the most important and most talked about place to list your local business. Getting citations from many of the sites below (as well as ratings) can help boost your business' listing in Google.

Yelp

The most popular social networking, directory and review site. Aside from counting as a citation for your business in the eyes of major search engines, this site can deliver quite a bit of traffic on it's own. However, business-owners using Yelp will need to learn to deal with the occasional nasty review.

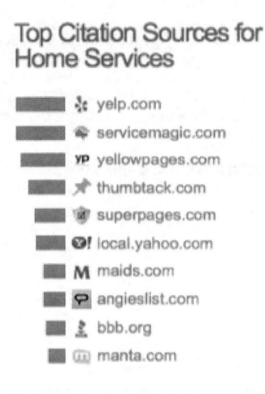

Top Citation Sources for
Home Services

- yelp.com
- servicemagic.com
- yellowpages.com
- thumbtack.com
- superpages.com
- local.yahoo.com
- maids.com
- angieslist.com
- bbb.org
- manta.com

Foursquare

A popular way to check-in to various locations using a smart phone. This can also provide a valuable citation for your local business.

Universal Business Listing

A local listing service – UBL.org (along with Localeze below) is one of the major players in the effort to only fill in your information once while getting listed on multiple yellow pages sites, directories and social networking/review sites. It saves time and effort but may be slower than going direct with the individual sites (see Localeze and InfoUSA below).

Yahoo Local
Yahoo's local directory tied to Yahoo Maps.

Local.com
Business listings, event listings, coupons and reviews.

CitySearch
One of the most authoritative local directories.

Bing Local
Bing's local business listing service integrated with maps of cities and towns.

CraigsList
Some recommend creating classifieds for your business on popular sites such as Craigslist. There's some disagreement over whether this is effective from an SEO point of view.

GetListed.org
Convenient way to identify where you are and are not listed in major directories. Provides referrals to Universal Business Listings and Localeze as well as consultants (if you need extra help).

dmoz (Open Diretory Project)
A free and authoritative index (in the eyes of Google) that is managed by volunteers. If you can get your business listed, this helps with an authoritative backlink (but not necessarily a local citation). It can be difficult to get a new listing due to the limited resources and large volumes of submissions.

Superpages
One of the many Internet Yellow Pages directories (IYP). Includes busi-

ness listings, people search, reviews and local deals.

Localeze
A multiple local listing service.

InfoUSA
A multiple local listings service.

Your local Chamber of Commerce
Joining your local chamber of commerce can often get you a business listing (and a citation for local SEO purposes).

InsiderPages
Local directory and rating site.

Merchant Circle
Local directory and rating site.

Best of the Web
A popular directory with free and paid listing options – specifically for local, they have a Best of the Web Local directory.

Yellowpages.com
Internet yellow pages (also YP.com).

Business.com
Business.com provides business information but also has a business directory.

Kudzu
Business review site (like Yelp).

Better Business Bureau
Your local Better Business Bureaus will usually charge for membership and provide a link to your business.

DexKnows
Business and people directory.

Acxiom
A major source of data for various yellow pages and directories – they don't take business submissions like some of the other data providers or multiple local listings services.

Your local newspaper's website
Getting an article, business listing or classified ad optimized with your local information and a link can provide a citation for your business.

Yellowbook.com
Internet yellow pages.

HotFrog
A business directory with free and fairly inexpensive paid listing options.

Crunchbase
A listing of technology companies that is user-generated.

Angie's List
Service provider directory.

Judy's Book
Local review site.

Jigsaw
Business people and company directory.

ibegin
US and Canadian business directory.

OpenList
Local directory with ratings.

wikimapia
Wiki-based directory of places including schools, businesses, and more – laid out on maps.

citysquares
Local business directory with ratings.

Infospace
Business and people listings.

magicyellow
A straightforward internet yellow pages directory.

whitepages.com
People and business listings.

Manta
Company profiles.

EZLocal
Local business listings and ratings.

BrownBook
Local business listings and ratings.

CityVoter
Vote for favorite businesses.

ShopCity
Local business listings.

YellowBot
Local listings and ratings.

MojoPages
Social networking and review site (like Yelp).

Tupalo.com
International social networking and review site.

Praized
Social networking and review site.

Panoramio
Pictures associated with maps. Geo tag images, upload to Panoramio and add them to your Google Places listings.

GetFave
Business directory, including featured listings (with additional content such as videos and pictures).

BizJournals
Business journal that includes business directories for certain US cities.

Tjoos
Online store listings and coupons,

JoeAnt
Website directory.

Zidster
Products, services or business listings.

TrueLocal
Business directory – seems to have sparse listings.

ZipLeaf
Network of international business directories.

WCities
Places and events for cities and towns, including ratings.

Naymz
Personal branding site.

Zoominfo
Database of people and companies.

Yellowikis
Wiki-based business directory.

gomylocal
Yellow pages/local directory.

Fast Pitch Network
Online business networking site.

City Slick
Free business directory.

Busiverse
Business directory.

yellowpages.lycos.com
A general directory.

Service Magic
Directory of service companies (includes a "seal of approval").

By securing these high quality citations you will boost your authority and highly improve your probability of ranking in the Google Map Listings. The next critical step is to get online reviews!

HOW TO GET ONLINE REVIEWS. REAL REVIEWS FROM YOUR REAL CUSTOMERS IN YOUR TRUE SERVICE AREA.

The next critical component for getting ranked on the Google Map, after you've claimed and optimized your listing, you've established your N.A.P. and you've developed your citations across the web, is obtaining reviews. You need to have real reviews from your real customers in your true service area.

First, I want to point out that you shouldn't fill the system with fake or fraudulent reviews. You do not want to create bogus accounts and post reviews to Google Map, Yelp, City Search, etc. just for the sake of saying you've got reviews. That's not going to help you. You need real reviews from your actual customers in your true service area.

You might be thinking "Well, how is that important?" or "How would Google know the difference?" Google is paying very close attention to the reviewer's profile.

If somebody is an active Google user and they've got a Gmail account, and they've got a YouTube channel, typically that's all connected to a Google profile.

Say that person with the active profile has had their account for seven years and actually happens to be located in your service area. If he or she writes you a review, it would be considered credible and will count in your favor. Now, if somebody creates a Google account with the sole intent of writing a review, it obviously is not credible and Google is capable of catching on to that. That account has no history associated with it and it was originated right at your office IP address. That review is going to be flagged as a bogus submission.

It is important to have an authentic strategy where you are connecting with real people who will write your reviews. You don't want to try and play the system. Google is fully aware, and so is Yelp and a number of other popular online review sites.

With that said, how can you get reviews? What kind of process will you need to actually get reviews from your real customers in your real service area? Here's the strategy that we advocate.

First of all, have some review cards printed up (a sample is referenced later in this chapter). It's basically just a simple document with your company logo, and a short and sweet thank you note.

We Hope You Are Satisfied With The Service We Provided Today.

All Purpose Plumbing

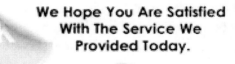

Positive reviews help us out, we would appreciate it if you would be so kind as to leave us a review on Google + Local. Please go to this URL and leave us a review.

http://www.allpurposeplumbing.com/reviews/

"Thanks so much for your business. We appreciate the opportunity to serve you. We'd love it if you would write us a review." Then give them a link to a page on your website where they can write you a review.

You will want to do some homework on the front end. Be sure you have a page on your website that is clearly meant for reviews: yourcompany.com/reviews. On that page you'll have links to the various places where people can write your reviews.

You'll want to have a link to your Google map listing, Yahoo local listing, Angie's List listing, City Search listing and any others that you may have. The reason you want to really have a variety of places where people can write those reviews is twofold.

Yes, you want to have a lot of reviews on the Google map. But, Google is also looking at the reviews that you have on other websites like Yelp and Angie's List. They're looking at the reviews that you have on Yellow Pages and on Insider pages and on Kudzu.

You need to diversify where you're getting reviews from your customers. It looks more authentic to have 12 on Google, 17 on YP.com and 13 on Kudzu, than it does if you just have 72 reviews on the Google map.

You want to make it easy and you want to give people options.

The other thing you want to pay bear in mind is that different people use different systems. I am personally a big Google user. If you sent me an email or gave me a card that said, "Please write me a review" and provide me with various options, I'm going to say, "OK, Google." Click Google. Write my review.

Some people, however, don't have Google accounts. They're not active Google users, but they may be really heavily involved in Angie's List or big-time reviewers on Yelp. They're going to have active accounts some-where. It would be much easier for them to write the reviews where they already have an existing account. The easier and more convenient you make it for people, the better. It's going to bode well in your favor.

Like we mentioned, Google is looking at the reviewer profile. If you only give them one option, and that's the Google map, but they happen to be a Yelp user without a Google account, they would have to go out of their way to create an account to write the review. This is not likely to happen. But, let's say they did decide to create an account. That review is not going to count for much because there's no active profile.

By providing options, the Yelp user that has a reputation for writing reviews and decides to write one for you is going to make a difference. That review is going to stick as opposed to being filtered. Make it easy for them to choose the one that's going to be easiest for them.

Now let's get back to the strategy. Phase one, print out review cards. Have your technicians hand them out after a service. "Hey, thanks for your business. I just want to leave this with you. If you'd be willing to write us a review and share your experience, we would really appreciate it." It's great. You're showing appreciation. You're holding yourself accountable because you're asking for feedback. By doing that on a consistent basis, you are likely to catch some fish.

The next thing you'll want to do, just to get a nice little bump in the number of reviews that you have, is to develop an email list of your circle of influence. Your circle of influence is going to be your most recent customers, the customers that have been using your services for quite some time, your family members, and your friends. People that you know, like, and trust, who would be willing to act on your behalf.

Put together that email list in an Excel sheet. It might be ten contacts, or it might be 700 contacts. Include , the names and email addresses of these folks. Then, use a tool like Constant Contact or MailChimp or another email marketing tool to send an email blast with the following message:

EMAIL SUBJECT: THANKS FOR YOUR BUSINESS!

Name,

I wanted to shoot you a quick email to thank you for your business and let you know how much we appreciate the opportunity to serve you!

Our goal is to provide 100% customer satisfaction and exceed your expectations every step of the way. I certainly hope that we did just that! If so, it would really help us out if you'd be willing to post a review for us online at one of your favorite online review sites. Below are a few direct links where you could write a public review about your experience with us:

• Google - https://plus.google.com/105923821769482824984
• Yelp - http://www.yelp.com/biz/carolina-deck-and-fence-charlotte
• Angie's List - http://www.angieslist.com/companylist/us/nc/charlotte/carolina-deck-and-fence-inc-reviews-336039.htm

Thank you again! We really appreciate your support!

Best Regards,
Luke Chapman
Carolina Deck & Fence

Again, save them the time of having to find the websites on their own by providing some links to the various places to where they can write reviews. By doing sending this email, you're going to create a little bump in your online review profiles. Again, reviews are important. Getting ten reviews on Google Maps is essential. It makes a huge difference in how you rank and it gives you a different perception in the mind of your consumers. You want to get to pass that ten review threshold almost immediately.

Doing that helps you get real reviews from real people that have real online profiles. Again, you want to have a systematic process in place where you are asking for reviews on a consistent basis from the customers that you are serving on a daily basis. The best way to do that is to request an email address from your customers, either at point of service or after service.

We have found that the best time to ask for that email address is at the point of booking the service. If you wait until after the service is rendered your technicians on-site will say "OK, thanks for the money, by the way give me your email address". They are going to say, "Why do you need my email address?" "Oh, because I want to ask you for a review or..." There is a lot of resistance to it at that point in the sales funnel.

However, if you move into the front where somebody calls in and says, "Hey I need to schedule a service, my house is flooded." You can respond, "We can get somebody out there right away. Let me gather your information." This is the perfect time to get the email address. Typically, you get their name, address, and the phone number. Well, you can just add one more step at that point and request an email address as well. You can tell them that it is so you can send a confirmation. That's how you start to develop a database of emails. We are going to talk about email marketing later in the book as part of your online marketing plan, but for this purpose, you need an email address so that you can send a message after service thanking them for their business and asking them to write you a review.

The number of reviews that you have from actual customers is going to increase exponentially if you repeat this process regularly. This is how you are going to start to really dominate the Google Map, because reviews and citations work in harmony for ranking.

SAMPLE REVIEW CARD

We Hope You Are Satisfied
With The Service We
Provided Today.

All Purpose Plumbing

Positive reviews help us out, we would appreciate
it if you would be so kind as to leave us a review on
Google + Local. Please go to this URL and leave us a review.

http://www.allpurposeplumbing.com/reviews/

SAMPLE REVIEW REQUEST EMAIL

Name,

I wanted to shoot you a quick email to thank you for your business and let you know how much we appreciate the opportunity to serve you!

Our goal is to provide 100% customer satisfaction and exceed your expectations every step of the way. I certainly hope that we did just that! If so, it would really help us out if you'd be willing to post a review for us online at one of your favorite online review sites. Below are a few direct links where you could write a public review about your experience with us:

• Google - https://plus.google.com/105923821769482824984
• Yelp - http://www.yelp.com/biz/carolina-deck-and-fence-charlotte
• Angie's List - http://www.angieslist.com/companylist/us/nc/charlotte/car
   olina-deck-and-fence-inc-reviews-336039.htm

Thank you again! We really appreciate your support!

Best Regards,
Luke Chapman, Carolina Deck & Fence

SAMPLE 'REVIEW US' LANDING PAGE FOR YOUR WEBSITE

If you follow these steps to properly claim your Google Map listing, develop your authority via citation development and put a systematic process in place to get real reviews from your real customers in your true service area, you will be well on your way to dominating the Google Map listings in your market.

7

WEBSITE CONVERSION FUNDAMENTALS - HOW TO ENSURE THAT YOUR WEBSITE CONVERTS VISITORS INTO LEADS IN THE FORM OF CALLS AND WEB SUBMISSIONS

This chapter is all about website conversion fundamentals; about how you need to set up your website, the messaging on your website, the navigational flow of your website, to ensure maximum conversion and profitability from your entire online marketing effort.

The way I look at it is, you can have the best Pay-Per-Click campaign, search engine optimization, and be ranked number one on the Google Map. But, if the content and the structure of your website isn't set up in a way that's compelling for users, then it doesn't give them a reason to choose you over the competition, and it doesn't give them the information that they need to easily say, "You're the company that I am going to call for help." It's just not going to do as well as it could. I want to talk about how we can take the traffic we're going to get from organic and Pay-Per-Click strategies, and make sure that the website is illustrating the correct message so we can maximize the profitability and revenue of our online marketing strategies.

Be real. I talked about how people resonate with real people. They like to see the company, the people that they are going to be talking with on the phone and that are going to be going out to their home. So, as often as you can, avoid stock photography. Get a picture of the owner, the team, and the front of the vehicle.

These things really draw people in and it gets them to feel see that they would be working with real people because that is the kind of business that people want to deal with. As for the content of your website, write messaging that draws them in and makes them connect. They're looking for a plumbing, roofing or pool company, so when they land on your homepage, the first message they see should enforce the fact that they can trust you. You should write something along the lines of, "Are you looking for a company that you can trust? Then you've come to the right place. We're operating on the same principles for the last 30 years: trust, innovation, and excellence."

Connect with them. Give them reasons to choose you and have a call-to-action, "Give us a call at this number for immediate service," or, "Click here to take advantage of our online specials and discounts." Remember, they've browsed around the internet and have seen that there are hundreds of companies that they can choose from.

Give them some compelling information about who you are and why they would want to choose you. Ask them to call now for an appointment, and then draw them into a section where they can get an offer or a special discount. This is is going to incentivize them to choose you and make that call right away.

When it comes to the copy on the website, you want to address their specific concerns. On the home page, write something generic, "Looking for a plumbing company?" On the water heater repair page, sympathize with them. "I know how frustrating it is when you need hot water and it is not coming through. You need to make sure that you've got hot water in your house. We can quickly get somebody out that understands water heaters and resolve the issue the first time."

Write that kind of messaging for each one of the pages on your website including a clear call to action after every block of text saying, "Call now to schedule your appointment," or, "Click here to reference one of our online coupons for a discount on your first service." Pull them deeper into your website with "About Us" links, special offers, and links to before-and-after images, especially for remodel type stuff.

Give them content that makes them think, "these guys know what they're doing," and draw them deeper and deeper into the website so they're more inclined to take the next step. Tell them why they should choose you over the competition. I talked about this in the "Message Market Media" chapter.

You should also, of course, have a web-form on each of the pages of your website or, at a minimum, on the "Contact Us" page. This is so that if they're not in the modality to pick up a phone, they can simply type in their name, email address, and phone number and let you contact them. Again, make sure that you've got your phone number on the top right-hand corner. You've got a clear call to action telling them what to do next on every page of your website, under every block of text.

Check out our reviews, download a coupon, look at our before-and-after photos. Explain why they should choose you. Leverage personality. Be authentic. Integrate your photos into your website. It really, really helps with conversion. Utilize your reviews, testimonials and videos. There's no reason you can't create a simple video for each of the pages on your website, explaining what the service is, and why your business can do it best. Some people are visual, they can see the content on the website, read it and feel fine. Other people are more audible and would prefer to hear the message. If you can spend the time to provide both text and video, it really helps with conversion. Give them external proof. Take them out to the review sites where they can preview testimonials on Angie's List, Google Maps, etc.

Show them what other people are saying, and you're going to significantly improve your conversion.

EXAMPLE OF A CONTRACTING SITE THAT IS BUILT TO CONVERT

Internet marketing involves a lot of little things that are performed in sequence to get people to call your company when they are in need of plumbing or HVAC service. At the end of the month, it all comes down to the amount of calls you received and how much business was booked, right?

1. Company logo should always be in the top left hand side of the page. Their logo here is the perfect size. Sometimes clients tell me they want their logo to be triple this size. The reality is that few searchers know you from your company name, so occupying too much space with just your logo is a waste of valuable webpage real estate.

2. Your phone number is VERY IMPORT¬ANT for plumbing and HVAC companies. It should be as close to the top right hand corner as possible. Make sure it's large and easy to find. Try not to make people search for your it. It's frustrating for searchers and you have just a few seconds for them to find it before they may move on to another website. People always look to the top of the page for that vital piece of info.

3. Professionally shot photos. For a small investment, you could and should have a professional photographer come in and take some photos. You will use them everywhere. DIY photography is ok, but a professional photo is so much better. Here, we placed Geno Caccia, the CEO of the company, in the top left hand of every page on the site with his hand out. This is a welcoming photo and combined with the family photo to the left of him, immediately gives the company a warm and welcoming look and feel.

4. A small blurb of text confirming the family-owned and operated company really brings it all together. People buy from people, not hidden companies. Personalize your website as much as possible. Your website is a marketing tool and it's job is lead capture and to bring down as many buying barriers as possible.

5. Main navigation. Your website's main navigation should be easy to find and the links should be clearly descriptive. Give people the option of moving around your website. One of Google's algorithms is how many pages a person visits and what their visit length was. Guide them down a path without confusing them. In other words, give them all the information they need in as few clicks as possible, but provide them the option of navigating around your site.

6. Some people want a way to contact you without calling. A contact form above the fold (the top half of the page) is great for capturing clients' info. In the case of James Caccia Plumb¬ing, they get a lot of form submissions on a monthly basis. Without the form, those clients may not have even contacted them. It's also a great tool for building a contact list for email marketing down the road.

7. Get to the point right away without going into too much detail. The first paragraph of your text should give you a brief introduction of who you are and what you do. You can go into further detail on your About Us page.

8. You can't see it here, but this area is a slider graphic. This three-window slider is a nice visual effect that adds movement to the page and delivers on three core services or important messages that you want people to know about.

9. Social media icons are a great tool because it allows potential visitors to see another side of your company. It's a great place to publish more videos and photos. Also, it's a great place to see how your company interacts with its community. From an SEO point of view, it helps build your company's social signal, something Google is paying more attention to. Social media is no longer just sexy marketing speak, it is a must when it comes to online marketing.

10. Don't forget about going mobile. The mobile web is huge and for the first time ever, ,mobile searching has passed desktop searching in the local market. It's only going to continue to grow. The important thing with mobile is to make it easy and to get all of the important information front and center. Make sure everything is only a click away and always have your 'call us' button on top.

8

MOBILE OPTIMIZATION - HOW TO OPTIMIZE YOUR WEBSITE FOR MOBILE VISITORS

More and more of your customers are searching for contractors & home service providers via mobile device. Here are just a few eye opening mobile stats that you should be aware of:

- 61% of local searches on a mobile phone result in a phone call. (Google, 2012)
- 52% of all mobile ads result in a phone call. (xAd, 2012)
    - o There are 7 billion people on Earth. 5.1 billion own a cell phone. 4.2 billion own a toothbrush. (Mobile Marketing Association Asia, 2011)
    - o It takes 90 minutes for the average person to respond to an email. It takes 90 seconds for the average person to respond to a text message. (CTIA.org, 2011)
    - o Mobile coupons get 10 times the redemption rate of traditional coupons. (Mobile Marketer, 2012)
    - o 91% of all smart phone users have their phone within arm's reach 24/7 – (Morgan Stanley, 2012)
    - o 44% of Facebook's 900 million monthly users access Facebook on their phones. These people are twice as active on Facebook as non-mobile users (Facebook, 2012)

o Mobile marketing will account for 15.2% of global online ad spend by 2016. (Berg Insight, 2012)

o It takes 26 hours for the average person to report a lost wallet. It takes 68 minutes for them to report a lost phone. (Unisys, 2012)

o 70% of all mobile searches result in action within 1 hour. 70% of online searches result in action in one month. (Mobile Marketer, 2012)

o 9 out of 10 mobile searches lead to action, over half leading to purchase. (Search Engine Land, 2012)

Mobile smartphones can access websites, as well as perform a multitude of other tasks, which is why they have become more of a necessity than a luxury these days. For you, as a plumbing or HVAC business owner, this provides a unique opportunity to connect with local customers via their mobile devices.

Before you start to develop a mobile arsenal to drive more inbound calls, you must first figure out who your mobile competitors are. It is important to know who you are up against in mobile marketing so you can plan your strategies accordingly.

To effectively do this, you need to identify your closest competitors and learn what mobile techniques they are using to generate their sales. First, find out which of your competitors have a mobile-optimized website. One quick and easy way to find out is to pull up their website on your mobile phone.

Did it load quickly? Was it easy to find their contact information and other details that consumers tend to look for while on-the-go? If so, they have invested in their business by making sure their mobile customers and prospects are taken care of.

Now, pull up your website on your mobile phone. If it's a nightmare, it's not your phone that is the problem, it's your website. This means you have been losing potential business.

Next, figure out which of your competitors are using text message marketing. If your competitors are doing it, they are probably telling the world to "text 123 to example." If you see promotions such as this, they are using text messaging to build a list of repeat customers.

This is one of the most cost-effective and results-oriented forms of marketing today. Text message marketing allows your competition to draw in local consumers with a great offer. Then, they send out occasional messages or coupon offers to keep them coming back to use their services.

Let's say one of your customers had plans to contact your business today after work, but they recently joined your closest competitors mobile list and had received a text coupon offer from them before they had the chance... Who do you think the customer will call?

There are many other forms of mobile marketing your competitors could be using to capture the attention of local consumers such as mobile SEO, QR codes and mobile apps.

If they are using these methods, it may be in your best interest to start researching how your business can do it even better.

ANALYZE YOUR CURRENT MOBILE MARKETING STATUS

What is your status when it comes to staying connected with local consumers using Mobile Marketing strategies?

Researching your competition is a necessary task if your goal is to become the local authority in your niche. But, it is equally important for you to analyze where your business currently stands in order to move forward.

Are you currently running a mobile marketing campaign, but not seeing the results you want? Or, do you want to start a mobile marketing campaign but keep putting it off because you don't know where to begin?

Every business in your local area is in a crucial fight for more customers and profits. Therefore, in order to enjoy a spike in sales, your company can no longer ignore the profitability of ramping up your mobile efforts.

Many business owners pump a lot of muscle in competing with similar businesses, while neglecting to take a close look at what they're doing. Analyzing your mobile status will help you figure out which weaknesses are holding you back and which strong points can help you win the war.

You need to understand where your past efforts have taken you, as well as what your future has in store for you based on where you stand today. For starters, it is crucial that you take note of what you are and aren't doing to generate more sales using mobile marketing.

Is your mobile website user-friendly? Does it load within seconds or take forever to render properly?

Does your mobile website have all of the relevant information on it that consumers look for while on the go?

Does your mobile website come up high in the rankings on mobile search engines, or is it nowhere to be found when local consumers perform a search for you "plumber + your city" or "AC repair + your city" on their mobile devices?

Have you started to build a text marketing list? If so, what are you currently doing with that list? Are you focused on building a trusting relationship or are you spamming them with offers on a daily basis and getting high rates of opt-outs?

Is your opt-in/call-to-action on all of your printed and web marketing materials?

Are you using QR codes as an additional method of increasing awareness about your business? Do you have your QR codes on all of your other marketing materials? Are you using them to direct traffic to your mobile website?

Do you currently use a mobile app to keep your audience engaged?
As you can see, there are a lot of things to consider when it comes to
making sure your business is on the right track toward beating your local
competition with mobile marketing.

SPY ON YOUR MOBILE MARKETING COMPETITORS

Do you want to know how your closest competitors are driving more
business by using mobile marketing? Just take a look at their campaign
yourself.

Mobile marketing has recently opened new doors for businesses that want
to market their products and services by using mobile phones as personal
mini-billboards. This has been enhanced by the fact that more and more
people own mobile devices, and use them to find local products, services
and businesses regularly.

To beat your competitors in the world of mobile marketing, you need to
know what they are doing to be ahead of the curve. Digital technology is
growing at astonishing rates and is not expected to slow down anytime
soon. This alone is causing many companies to be left behind when it
comes to new-age technology.

Spying on your competitors' mobile marketing initiatives may seem like a
daunting task, but it's not. In fact, all you need to do is identify which are
taking most of your customers and let the research begin.

You should begin by visiting their mobile websites on your phone. Go
through the websites and take note of the look and feel, the features and
the traffic flow. Although your goal is NOT to copy exactly what they're
doing, you could get a few pointers for your own mobile website.

Next, find out how their text message marketing campaigns operate simply
by joining their mobile list. They probably have a text call-to-action placed
everywhere, so opt-in and pay close attention to what happens throughout
the entire process. This is the perfect way to get a first-hand look at their

services, products, and promotions.

Are your competitors using QR codes to generate interest in their business? If so, whip out your mobile phone and scan their codes to see what lies behind them. Where do the QR codes take you? What type of incentives are they offering to get people to scan them?

Another thing you can look into is your competitors' mobile applications. Download their apps and see what they're offering and how user-friendly they are.

The information you gain from your research should be used solely to set up your mobile marketing campaign that will not only beat your competitors, but will also attract new customers and keep them loyal to your business.

Spying on your competitors is not illegal, but there are limits you should follow to remain fair. Under no circumstances should you use unethical measures to jeopardize your competition in your quest for mobile marketing.

MAKE CUSTOMERS CALL YOUR PLUMBING BUSINESS WITH MOBILE MARKETING

The secret to beating your competitors in the business is making your company more interesting to your target audience. There are several ways to do this using mobile marketing if you plan ahead, focus on the right things, and maintain your campaigns over time.

As much as you would like to boot your local competitors out of the picture, the fact is that a lot of them will probably be using some of the same mobile marketing methods as you are.

So, your main focus should be geared toward making your customers choose your business over theirs. This is fairly easy to do if your efforts are consistent and persistent.

It is up to you which tools you use to work positively toward attracting new customers and keeping the ones you already have.

Here are a few tips that can work in your favor and help local consumers choose you:

- You need to have a good website that is mobile-friendly and easily ac cessible by mobile phone users in your area. People are using their mobile phones to access the web to search for local products and ser vices while on the go. Make sure your site loads quickly, gives them the exact information they need, and is easy to navigate.
- If you choose to start a text message marketing campaign, make sure your text messages offer great value, relay a clear message, and are short and informative. Also, be sure to send messages out consistently, yet conservatively. Create a careful balance that makes sense for your business and your target audience. Need a boost in getting new mobile subscribers? Give your customers and prospects a great incentive in exchange for opting-in and watch your list grow exponentially.
- Consumers love businesses who stay "on top" of the digital age. They expect you to have a website, to actively involved in their favorite social media outlets, and to be easily accessible from their mobile devices. Have a mobile app developed to aid in keeping your local consumers connected with your business. Implement the use of QR codes as a way to keep your local consumers engaged and provide them with "instant gratification."
- Mobile SEO should be used effectively to attract qualified traffic to your website. Mobile users search for local products and services constantly on their mobile devices when on-the-go. If your business does not rank in the results, there is major potential profit leak left for your competitors to scoop up.

If somebody goes online, searches for your services, and gets to your web-site, they probably want to just get the basic information.

They probably are not interested in learning a ton of informaton about you. They simply want to find who you are, where you're located, what your services are, and then press a button to call you. I have an example of a mobile version of a plumbing site where they can just get the basic information, hit that "Call Us" button, and they're on the phone with you. You should absolutely set up a mobile version of your site, don't overcomplicate it, and give the basic information.

Now that you have your website conversion fundamentals in order and have a proactive Mobile Marketing plan, you can start to think about Social Media Marketing.

9

SOCIAL MEDIA MARKETING
HOW TO LEVERAGE SOCIAL MEDIA (FACEBOOK, TWITTER, GOOGLE+, LINKEDIN & OTHER SOCIAL PLATFORMS) FOR MAXIMUM EFFECT IN YOUR CONTRACTING/HOME SERVICES BUSINESS.

There is a lot of BUZZ around Social Media (Facebook, Twitter, Google Buzz, YouTube, LinkedIn), but how can it be leveraged by a Plumbing Contractor? How can you use social media to grow your contracting or home services business?

In this chapter we are going to cover social media marketing for your home services business. I hope that by now, you've learned a lot about how to position your company online, how to rank well on the organic listings on the Google Map, and how to rank well in the organic non paid listings. Now, we're going to talk about social media marketing, and how you can utilize social media tools like Facebook, Twitter, Google+, and LinkedIn to grow your business.

As I talk to contractors throughout the country about internet marketing and social media, I tend to get a puzzled look. The question is, "How in the world does all of this social media stuff apply to my business? How can I possibly use Facebook in a way that would help me grow my revenues, grow my service calls, and get more repeat business?"

I'd like to try and bridge the gap on where the lowest "hanging fruit" for social media is in your plumbing or HVAC business by asking, "What's your number one source of business today" Just stop and think, where does most of our revenue come from? You'll quickly come to the conclusion that your number one source of revenue is repeated and referral business.

= More Repeat Business & More Referrals

The lifeblood of any service business is your existing customers returning for services over time, and your existing customers referring you to their friends and family. If social media is harnessed correctly, it gives you the ability to take that repeat and referral business, inject it with steroids, and take it to a whole new level.

Let me explain why I feel that it's a great place for you to really connect with your customers and get more repeat and referral business. Just a couple of Facebook stats:

Facebook currently has 1.6 billion users.
The average user has 135 friends, and checks in between 6 and 9 times per day.

If you can get your real customers, current and past, your sphere of influence, to connect with you on social media, Facebook, Twitter and/or Google+, your business is exposed to their 135 friends as soon as they "like" and follow your page.

It's almost as if they'd sent an email, or they'd sent a text message out to all their friends saying, " I used this great contractor in our area. The next time you need their services, why don't you think about them?" It's extremely powerful to gain exposure to their sphere of influence.

Another major advantage is that they've given you permission to remain top-of-mind with them. The average user, like I said, checks in between 6 and 9 times per day. They login to check out the updates on their Facebook wall and to see the updates of all the companies and people they have liked or are friends with. If you're posting updates to your social media profiles, the people who have liked your page are going to see the new content whenever they login.

They are going to see an update and your logo. They're going to see some special offer or promotion, and it's going to peak their interest. Next time they need your services, who do you think they're going to call?

There is a higher probability for them to use you again, and refer you to their friends, because they remember youyou and had a good experience with . They know who you are. You've remained top-of-mind. If you look at major companies like Coca Cola, Pepsi, and Lay's, they spend billions of dollars a year on advertising and promotions; TV, radio, print. What's the whole thought process behind that? They're developing their brand, so they can maintain what we call "TOMA," top of mind awareness. Leveraging social media inside your existing sphere of influence is a great way to tap into that top-of-mind awareness.

Where should you start? Where can you start using social media, with all of the different platforms out there? With so many different social media tools, what should you be using?

In chapter two, we talked about having a blog and putting out consistent updates. Well, blogging ties very nicely to your social media strategy. These are the social media profiles you definitely want to have set up and ready to roll in your business.

Let's talk strategy before we get into the granular details. Talk about high level. How do you leverage social media and how do you gain that initial following?

Well, first of all, you want to utilize email to get initial engagement. Having an active social media profile with daily updates is not worth a hill of beans if you don't have likes or viewers.

- Facebook Business Page
- Twitter
- LinkedIn
- YouTube
- Google Plus
- Blog

Now, at the same time, if you have thousands of irrelevant people that have pressed like on your website or on your Facebook profile, it's not going to work to your advantage if they're not people in your area. They're not homeowners. They're not the target market that we discussed in the marketing fundamentals.

You want to make sure that you have a strategy to get your real customers and your true service area engaged with you in social media. You should leverage email to engage your customers to get to your social media profiles. We take a multiple-step process.

The first thing you want to do is build that list or go into your customer relationship management system, if you have one, and export the name and email addresses of your customers. Current customers, past customers, sphere of influence of your friends, your business partners, the people that you do business with, and put them into an email.

Queue up a nice little message that says, "Hey, we appreciate your business. We appreciate your relationship over the years. We're getting active in social media and would love to have you engage with us. Please go to facebook.com," and give them a direct link to your Facebook page, "and press the like button."

There are a couple of things you can do. You can offer them an incentive, something of value like a coupon or a discount. Or, if you feel like you've got an active customer base that knows who you are and likes you, just ask them to do it as a favor.

You'll be able to start building that following. Now, you don't want to stop there. You don't want to just send one email out that says, "We're on social media." You now want to build it as part of your business.

In the Google Maps Optimization chapter, I talked about having an email go out after service, thanking the customer for their business and asking them to go ahead and write a review for you on one of the various online directory sites.

Well, there's no reason you couldn't send a subsequent email to that contact, maybe a day or two days later, that says, "By the way, we're actively involved in social media and would love it if you would engage with us." Then give them a direct link to your social media profiles where they can press like, subscribe, and follow to start engaging with you on social media.

The key is that it needs to be an automated process where you're typing your customer's name and their email address. These emails go out to everybody that you serve without any hiccups, without any potential for dropping the ball. If you don't do it consistently, you won't get a true following and you won't get your real customers engaging with you on these social media platforms.

That's step one. Leverage email to build that initial engagement and that following of your real customers. Remember, we want authentic customers, and not just throwaway links and subscribers.

Once you've got that part squared away, you have got to think about what are you going to post. What information are you going to put up and how frequently? You should post to your social media profiles once a day. If that seems like too much for your business, post once a week at a very minimum.

These should be informative posts. It should not be a sales pitch. It should not be, "Here's 10-percent off your next service."

You can do that every now and then but more than 80% of the time it should just be social content: "Here's a picture of a kitchen that we remodeled", "This is what's going on in our market", "Here's a picture of us at the latest home show.", etc.

Keep it informational, keep it relevant, keep it social, and then you have to engage. Social media isn't a one-way dialogue. You shouldn't be going to your social media profiles and pushing out updates that don't have any engagement. You shouldn't just be posting. You should be trying to get people to reply to your post: "Hey, that was funny", or "That's a beautiful picture", or "Thanks for that great tip," all of which you can reply back to. Then, listen to what your fans are saying. Once you've got a flow – you've got 50, 70, 100 or a couple of thousand people that have liked you – you are going to be able to hear what they are saying as well. They might post something that's totally irrelevant to you, like "Hey, tomorrow's Billy's birthday." There is no reason that your organization couldn't reach out and say, "Hey, wish Billy a happy birthday for us!", from your company. They will think, "Wow, this is a company that cares. This is a company that's real and authentic."

Engaging in social media is probably the lost art. Most people that use social media just post one-way messages, which is not the idea. It's a social

platform, so there should be conversation. There should be dialogue.
The next thing you want to do is to develop your brand and make sure that
you enhance the bio section on each one of these profiles. Within Facebook, Twitter, LinkedIn and Google+, you will have the option to fill in an
'About Us' or bio section. Write some interesting information about your
business there.

Take the information from the 'About Us' page on your website where you
talk about where you guys were founded, why you started the business, the
service that you offer, etc. and pop that into the bio section on your social
media profiles.

You also have the ability to put an icon on each one of these social profiles, and you want to make sure that you're using an image that represents
your business. It can either be a head shot of the owner or it can be a logo.

Below is an example of a few social media icon options from good to bad.

Good	**Good**	**Bad**	**Very Bad**
ompany Logo, even better if you are a well	Mary Thompson President Mr. Rooter	Glad you like shaggy, and maybe it's your	Drinking a beer while giving the middle finger.

If your personality represents your brand, then it's not a bad idea to use a
nice head shot so that people resonate with you. People tend to buy from
individuals more than they buy from businesses because a business is an
anonymous entity and a person is someone that they feel they can get to
know, like and trust.

Don't be like our bad examples, "shaggy" or the "drunk contractor." Don't
put a picture of yourself in a t-shirt with a beard grown out. Be professional. Represent yourself as an important part of the business. Stick with

the examples on the left – the logo and/or the professional head shot, as opposed to the shaggy or a weekend photo of you doing something crude and lascivious.

It's all about branding, so make sure that you're leveraging the header graphic and the image icon. If there is an option for you to customize the background, do it!. You want to make sure that you've got the elements that marry up with the overall branding of your business.

Make sure everything on your social media profiles is consistent with your website. On your website, you've got a color scheme, a logo, and maybe you've got brochures that are made up. Make sure that there's a consistent flow, look, feel, and color scheme on all of your social media profiles, website and offline materials.

Don't forget to have a plan; how often are we going to post? What types of posts are we going to put out there? How are we going to engage our customers? What social media profiles are we going to be involved with? Remember in chapter two we talked about the fundamentals of your marketing plan (market, message & media). You need to make sure that you have a clear understanding of who your customer is and who your ideal customer is. Then, make sure that you are crafting a message that will resonate with that particular customer. You need to think about all of these things as part of your social media strategy.

Don't just dive in. A common mistake would be to just setup the profile and start posting with no thought process or plan behind it. Think about it. What pages are you going to be on? What message are you going to put out? What color scheme are you going to use? Set all of that up and then get very specific about who your target is. Is your client the commercial type? Is your client a residential type?

One solid method is to schedule your post types:

Monday, Wednesday and Friday are the days that you are going to put up tips; Ex. what to do when the toilet starts to backup; what to do in the event of a plumbing emergency; why you should consider tank versus tankless, etc.

Tuesday and Thursday, you'll post photos; pictures of really interesting things relative to your business; pictures of nicely renovated bathrooms; pictures of silly things like a gummy bear coming out of a faucet; pictures that are interactive.

Saturday and Sunday you post coupons

I am not saying this is the editorial calendar you should follow. However, the point is to make it easy for yourself so that you know what is going up and when. You can be streamlined and it can be automated.

When we talked about the blog in the SEO chapter, we went over leveraging content. Because that content is king, you have to be creating updated information on a consistent basis. This content can go up in various places. As you post a new piece of content, it can go to your Facebook and Twitter pages automatically. It can go straight out to Pinterest if it has a photo included, and you can take your blog content and syndicate it to recreate great social media content.

Remember, content isn't necessarily just written text. You are a an expert on your craft. You know things that the average consumer doesn't, such as what to do in the event of a plumbing emergency, why somebody would want to consider tank versus tankless, or why somebody would want to consider trenchless sewer replacement.

You can either sit down and write about it, you can take an audio recorder and record yourself talking about it, or if you're comfortable on video, you can break out the camera phone and shoot a video talking about an issue that your ideal consumer may be facing.

That one piece of content can serve multiple functions. The first function can be posting videos up on the social media, on websites like YouTube, Vimeo, and Vine, where you can upload interesting clips and videos.

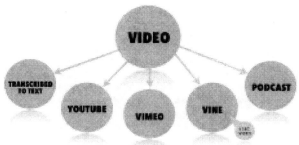

One video post can result in several forms of content.

You can also take that video and have it transcribed using a service like castingwords.com. There are various transcription services. That video of you talking about the benefits of tankless can now be transcribed into text, which may then be used as a blog post and be syndicated into your social media profiles. Another step beyond that is using that same audio and turning it into an audio podcast that you can have hosted on your website.

There are a lot of things you could do, to take your content and work with the modality that you're most comfortable with. Some people like to write. Some people like to talk. Some people like to be on video. Figure out what you are most comfortable with and run with that. This is how you create social media content for your online marketing plan.

Remember, educational content that's published in multiple places gives you industry expert status. By publishing and getting picked up in the PHCC, the local newspaper or a reputable blog, you are considered an expert. This is going to drive your credibility, which in turn, will result in more referrals.

I want to give you some examples of good social media posts.

The following example is a great tip for preventative maintenance. It's,

"Never flush your Kleenex tissues. The paper fiber does not disintegrate like toilet paper, and it causes clogging in your toilet." Then, of course, a shortened link back to the website, an ow.ly. The point is to give a quick tip like that once a day, keeping you top-of-mind and helping you to put out fresh, relevant content.

Powell's Plumbing @PowellsPlumbing   27 mins
Never flush your Kleenex tissues. The paper fibers do not
disintegrate like toilet paper causing clogs in your toilet. ow.ly/hP0Y9
Collapse ← Reply ⇄ Retweet ★ Favorite ••• More

1:45 p.m. - Feb 18, 2013 · Details

Here's another example. You wrote a post, and you're using a tool like Hoot Sweet. It can grab that RSS feed and automatically have that post hit your social media profile. If there's a new blog post, you can post something like "five questions to ask a plumber before any repairs," and of course a link to where the blog is posted.

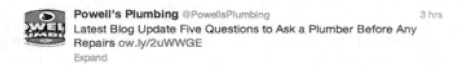

Powell's Plumbing @PowellsPlumbing   3 hrs
Latest Blog Update Five Questions to Ask a Plumber Before Any
Repairs ow.ly/2uWWGE
Expand

Here's an example of how you can do something interesting with pictures. In the picture below they have plungers that are being used as hangers. It says, "A bit of plunger ingenuity. Need extra hanger space? Grab a plunger." You'd be amazed the things you can do with pictures. There's 200 percent more engagement with photos on Facebook, than there is with text.

It's easy to find an interesting picture like this, post it with a quick little quip, and get some great engagement from your followers on social media. Another sample, "Don't know how to get rid of scratches in your porcelain sink? Here's what you can do." Then they provide 23 tips to save time and money, and includes information on how you can seal porcelain sinks and fix metal scratches. This is a great place to share information and post valuable content that your consumer might find interesting and use to their benefit.

WHAT NOT TO POST:

1. Use the 80/20 rule for marketing messages, put out 80% information and 20% marketing.

2. Keep it business related. Your political and religious beliefs are never a good mix with business.

3. Photos of your kids playing tee ball are good, but don't let it dominate your page.

4. Keep your vacation photos on your personal social sites.

5. Keep your business opinions, beliefs, and interests to yourself.

Sometimes knowing what not to post is more important than knowing what to post, because the natural tendency is to go to these social media profiles, and just post promotional material. So, don't post a coupon every single time you log in. If you do that, everybody that liked or subscribed to your page will start to disappear before you know it. They'll stop subscribing, they'll unlike you, and they'll unfriend you.

You have to use the 80-20 rule for messaging: 80 percent informational and fun stuff, and only 20 percent should be promotional.

Try and keep it business related. You don't want to get into your political and religious beliefs, because if somebody disagrees with you, you can create a negative atmosphere. That's not something you want to do on your business profiles. You've got a personal profile for a reason. If you want to put your religious and political beliefs there, knock yourself out. Just keep it off of your business pages.

You may not necessarily want to put too many photos of your kids on your page, even though if you're a personality brand. Don't let your kids and your family be the dominant positioning behind your business profile page. Obviously, keep your vacation photos and again, your opinions and beliefs, off your business page. Family photos are another thing that should be kept primarily on your personal profile.

WHEN AND HOW TO ENGAGE

We talked about asking your customers to 'like you' on Facebook, and asking your customers to write testimonials. We also talked about inter- action and responding to your customer's actions. "Hey, thanks so much for the follow. We appreciate it." Or, if they write you a testimonial, make sure you blow that up.

Not only should you say thank you, but you should also share it. "Hey, Jean, thanks so much for the positive testimonial. We appreciate your feedback. We appreciate your business, and this is what keeps us going. This is what we're in this business for." Then, you could take that testimo- nial and put it on your website, or embed it on your website through the various widgets and short codes that Facebook provides.

For example, you make a post saying, "Because tankless water heaters provide hot water only when it's needed, they save up to 40 percent of your energy bill." Then, one of your followers says, "How long do tank- less water heaters last?" This is your engagement. You want people to ask questions, and then you want to be able to talk back.

You can write, "Typically, 15 to 20 years. Have you been thinking about installing one in your home?", "I have, but I'm not sure how to get start- ed." You can say, "Take a look at the tankless page on our website. Let's schedule a time to talk, so I can show you all the benefits of going tank- less."

This is just a way to put out relevant content, and if you're paying atten- tion to your feed, you can turn it into some great conversation. Again, you want to be active on social media. It's a great way to get repeat or referral business. You need to be on Facebook, LinkedIn, Twitter, YouTube, and Google Plus. You want to utilize email marketing to gain that initial fol- lowing, and then post updates that are informative and not sales-oriented on a consistent basis, and engage.

If you do this regularly and correctly, you're going to grow a nice following of real customers in your true service area. You're going to remain top-of-mind and it's going to help you grow your business in terms of the lifeblood of your organization, which is repeat and referral business.

EXAMPLE OF A CUSTOMIZED FACEBOOK PAGE:

EXAMPLE OF BANDED TWITTER PROFILE:

**For more details on how you can leverage Social Media and a video
explaining these concepts in more depth
go to www.contractorseo.net/social**

10

VIDEO MARKETING –
HOW YOU CAN TAP INTO THE POWER OF YOUTUBE AND OTHER VIDEO SHARING WEBSITES TO ENHANCE YOUR VISIBILITY AND DRIVE BETTER CONVERSION

Did you know that YouTube is the 2nd most used search engine (ahead of Bing & Yahoo)? Most contractors are so focused on search engine optimization, but neglect the opportunities that video and YouTube provide. Implementing a Video Marketing Strategy for your business can get you additional placement in the search results for your plumbing keywords, enhance the effectiveness of your SEO efforts and improve visitor conversion.

There are a number of reasons that you should engage in Video Marketing for your contracting business. The primary reason is that it's going to increase your exposure on the search engines, giving you more placeholders for the keywords that are most important to you. It's going to enhance your SEO effort by driving great visitors to your website and creating relevant links to your website, improving conversion. Once somebody gets to your website, if there is good video on the home page and the subpages, that is going to resonate deeper with your potential customers. It will help convert those visitors from just browsing around page to actually picking up the phone and calling your office.

Again, YouTube is the second most used search engine that there is. Obviously, Google is number one. One would think that Bing and Yahoo would be the other major search engines, but that isn't the case.

There is significantly less videos than there are web pages on the Internet. So, creating relevant and quality video content for YouTube and other video sharing sites is a really huge opportunity. These videos will help you to connect with people and answer their questions when they're looking for information on what you do.

I talked about the fact that you can now show up in search engines with an image next to it, and you can obtain multiple place holders on Google for the keywords that are most important to you. Here is a screenshot just visually representing what that means.

This company, Shamrock Plumbing in Orlando, really likes to focus on re piping. This company is the go-to re piping company in that area. If we type in a search on Google for Orlando re piping, you'll see that his video shows up on page one with a few listings and an image icon. If you click that link, it takes you straight to a video where he's talking about why you should re pipe your house, what options you have, and why you should choose his company for the job.

If you do this right and you optimize your videos correctly (I'm going to showing you exactly how in this chapter), you can start to have your video show up in the natural search on Google, which is extremely powerful. It also gives you the opportunity to have more placeholders, for the various services that you provide.

In this case, his website is optimized for Orlando re piping. The website and his videos show up in organic search in a couple of different pages. You can see examples of this through a variety of keywords. Not only will your website show up, but your video that's been correctly optimized can show up in that search as well.

Another example is a company that operates in the Easton, Pennsylvania area. If you type in "Easton sump pump repair," you will find that the website ranks first, followed directly by a video. Whether your video ranks number one, number two, or number three, most of the time you'll notice that the video gets a much higher click through rate.

This is because there is a large image displaying what that video is. Where are you going to click? A static piece of text or the image? A lot of attention goes to those video results. If you do what I'm going to be explaining throughout this chapter, you'll know how to incorporate these types of videos for your services, and optimize them to show up just like this in your market.

VIDEO HELPS WITH YOUR OVERALL SEO EFFORT

The other thing that we can accomplish with video is the enhancement of our SEO efforts. As covered in the SEO chapter, links are critical for ranking. By creating good video content, you have the ability to drive inbound links to your website from high level video sites like YouTube, Vimeo, and Metacafe.

Again, you don't want to have just the generic Home, About Us, Our Services, Contact Us pages on your website. You want to have a page for each of your core services and products. Videos that link to those pages is going to help with that SEO effort. Also, you're going to find that video content on your website, and on the pages of your site, actually reduces your bounce rate and improves the visitors' time on site.

These are SEO factors. 'Bounce rate' refers to somebody getting to your

page and clicking back immediately, or browsing away. Google understands those actions as the page not being relevant to that search.
If the majority of the people that get to your site click off and leave right away, your bounce rate is high, and Google is going to start to show you less prominently in their results. That's part of the Google algorithm. The other factor is the amount of time spent on the site. If somebody gets to your page, stays there for ten seconds, and then moves on, the visit might not get treated like a bounce, but Google is looking at the length on the site.

If you have a video and a visitor takes the time to watch it in its entirety, that's improving your website visit length statistics. Even if they only watch a couple seconds of the video, you have captured their attention long enough that Google is going to see that your site is relevant.

Don't get confused by the notion that having video on your page automatically improves your SEO. That's not necessarily the case. But, having people stay on your page longer and not bounce off does impact SEO. Here's an example of how you can drive some links with your videos.

Now, let's go deeper into this. Here's an example of the YouTube channel on "The Clean Plumbers", which is a plumbing company in Tampa. You can see in the description area that I am pointing to on the screen, that they have included a link:

TheCleanPlumbers.com. This link now connects you from YouTube to their site, and that's a relevant high impact link. You can do the same thing. I would suggest that you do not link to the home page, but rather to the specific subpage related to the video, like the water heater repair or the drain cleaning page. Here's an example, Shamrock Plumbing again. We looked at his video in surf for re piping.

Now, if you got to the Shamrock Plumbing website, and you will see a nice video of the owner right underneath the first block of text. If you are in the market for plumbing or HVAC services, you're most likely going to watch that video on the home page. Again, this is how you improve time on site and the bounce rate.

People like to watch videos. It's very rare, that you're going to see a video on subpages, but you'll find that if you do have that video content on the re pipe or the water heater repair page, people will take a couple minutes to watch it. Even if it is just because it's unexpected and it's more interesting than text. People enjoy listening to someone explain the topic that they are researching.

Here's just another example. I always recommend that your home page be above the fold.

Above the fold, meaning that you don't have to scroll down to see the most important information. You would only need to pull up the page and to see that the video shows up, above the fold. You will want to do the same, providing an intro video about who you are and what you do. Again, having that is going to improve on-page site time and reduce your bounce rate.

Another benefit that we have talked about is the fact that video gives you more placement in search. It's going to give you better search engine optimization because you get the links from the video sites, you're improving your time on site, and reducing your bounce rate. The other benefit of video that is probably even more powerful than anything, is that it's going to improve conversion.

You can have the best SEO strategy in the world, by driving hundreds of people that are looking for your services to your home page or to your subpage on a daily basis. But, if it's not converting and if people aren't picking up the phone and calling to hire you for your services after they visit your site, you're missing a major opportunity.

One of the main things that having intelligent video on your site is going to do is that it's going to improve conversion. The fact is that video clips resonate with people. They like it because it gives them the chance to get to know and trust you before they call you, especially if you follow my strategy rather than creating a super corporate video. If you create authentic video of your team, the owner or your service manager talking directly to the camera, connecting with you on an emotional level, answering questions and giving a strong call to action, your conversion rate will improve.

It also gives you the ability to connect with different modalities. Everybody thinks in a different way. Some people are readers and will read all of the content on a page. Some people are listeners, so if there's the opportunity to listen to something rather than read, they'll choose to listen. Other people like something visual. By having video on your website, combined with text (I'm not saying to abandon text), you have the opportunity to connect with every type of person. Some people will watch the video and only connect with that, because they wouldn't take the time to read a plain text web page.

Here's a company in Brooklyn, New York. Upon visiting their website, you will see both the text and a video from the owner of Petri Plumbing. If you watch the video, and if he says something that's relevant to you that makes me feel connected, you may think, "Man, this is a real guy. He runs an authentic plumbing company and he's going to make sure that he provides good quality service. He really stands behind his product."

Do you think you would be more apt to call him over somebody who doesn't have that type of messaging on their website? Video on the site is going to improve conversion rates. It's going to make your phone ring more.

How can we leverage video? We understand that it's powerful, it's going to improve your SEO, it's going to help us get better placement on the search engines, and it could potentially help with conversion. How can we expand upon this?

What we want to do is create simple videos about your company, your services, and the most frequently asked questions. You are then going to upload those videos to YouTube and other video sharing sites, and syndicate them to your website and social media profiles.

What type of video should you create? Like I keep saying, "People resonate with people." Keep it simple, be real and be personable. Put your real face on the camera, or the face of someone that represents your company. Be frank and to the point. It doesn't have to be a 20 minute video. An appropriate length would be 30 seconds to 3 minutes long, enough to get the message across.

Don't overthink it. Don't feel like you have to go all out and hire a high end production crew, or go out and buy a HD camera in order to make this happen. The reality is, you can create video clips using technology that you already have. If you've got an smartphone or a webcam, you have the ability to create video content that will work for your website.

You don't need high end editing software either. YouTube gives you the ability to upload regular video and edit it right within the system. By edit, I mean cropping and tailoring the video to begin and end where you wish. You can put your phone number down in the bottom area of the video as well as a link to your website. Or, you can use a simple editing software like iMovie (free with Macintosh computers) and Movie Maker (free with the PC).

Using the technology that you already have, stand in front of a company truck or a sign with your logo, and talk to the camera; talk with the people that are visiting your website, because that's going to stick with them. What kind of videos should you create? You can create just about anything you want. But, the ones that are going to be most relevant are the ones that pertain to your services.

The first video that I recommend you make is an introduction for your website. This can be as simple as, "Thank you so much for visiting the XYZ Company website. We specialize in providing XYZ services to the XYZ area. These are the things that make us unique and why people tend to choose us. We'd love the opportunity to serve you. Give us a call right away at the number below, and we can send somebody to your house to resolve your XYZ issue right away."

A simple video along those lines should be the first step of your plan. It's a necessity.

The other videos that you want to create should be about your primary services. This ties in well with the SEO strategy discussed previously. You want to make sure you have a page on your website for each one of the services that you provide.

So, you don't simply provide plumbing services. You've got emergency plumbing, drain cleaning, water heater repair, tankless water heater installation, bath remodeling, and more. If you're an HVAC company, you've got AC repair, AC installation, vent cleaning, etc. Make a list of the services that you want to attract more business for and shoot a brief video about each.

The other very powerful piece of content that you should incorporate, but should be phase two, would be your frequently asked questions, or FAQ. Make a list of the questions that people tend to ask and create a little video about it.

Ex. What to do in the event of a plumbing emergency; why you would want to consider tank versus tankless water heaters; the benefits of trenchless sewer replacement.

This is common information to you, but the average consumer doesn't know. Creating a little video providing answers to these frequently asked questions makes for great video content for your YouTube channel, to be syndicated on your social media profiles, and/or uploaded to your blog on your website.

Now that we know what types of videos we want to create and how to create them, what should we say? Should we have a script? Should we wing it? You want to be natural, you want to be authentic, and you want to be real. Some people have to have a script because they don't feel comfortable doing video outside of a scripted methodology. But, if there is any way you can get in front of a camera and speak naturally like you would to a customer in person about your services, that's going to work best.

Here is a simple script you can follow: "At XYZ Company, we provide a full range of XYZ services (to the specific area, whatever area you're in, or whatever service this video is about)." Have a brief description of what you do in that area, and then, "If you're in need of this service in your area, we can help. Call our office today at 555-5555."

If you are a plumber specializing in drain cleaning or your emergency plumbing, your page might say, "At Tom's Plumbing, we are experts in emergency plumbing services. When you've got a plumbing emergency, you need somebody that can get out to your house right away. You don't want to sit around. You don't want to have to call 10 different companies. You just want to feel confident that who you call is going to get to you within a reasonable period of time.

We are going to resolve the issue and we are not going to overcharge you. We specialize in providing emergency plumbing services to the area. We have technicians that can get out to your home within 30 minutes to an hour, and we'll make sure that you get priced fairly. If you'd like to talk with us and you would like to have us get a technician to you right away, give us a call. You can reach us at 555-5555. As a matter of fact, if you reference this coupon code "Emergency Plumbing Video" we'll knock $20.00 off your repair."

A simple video like that for each one of your services should always include the call to action telling them what to do. Also, if you feel comfortable with it, referencing a discount could go a long way.

Don't over think this. Think about the core services that you offer. Shoot a quick 30 second to one and a half minute video about each and you're ready to roll.

WHAT TO DO WITH YOUR VIDEO CONTENT
What are you going to do with the videos once you've got them? Now that you have completed shooting your videos, what you want to do is setup a YouTube channel.

You can do this by going to YouTube.com. You want to upload your video, name it correctly and intelligently, putting it in terms that somebody is going to search for it in. If somebody is looking for drain cleaning services, they are going to type in "your city drain cleaning services." You want to name the video using your keywords.

When you upload it to YouTube, you want to title it "Denver drain cleaning specialists" or "Denver drain cleaning services" and then put a description with a link to your site. "Visit us online at yourcompany.com/draincleaning" and then include a description about what you do, briefly outlining what was said in your video.

SOME YOUTUBE BEST PRACTICES

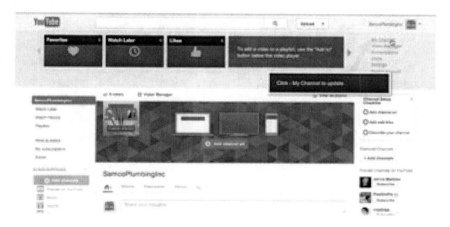

When you setup your channel, make sure that you give it a "city plus service, name of your company" title, instead of just your company name. You are also going to add tags with keywords to it. Don't just leave the tag area blank.

Make sure you use your name, address and phone number in every description on your YouTube channel because this is a good citation source.

As covered in the Google Maps optimization chapter, citation development is critical (having your company name, address and phone number referenced consistently across the web). This is a great place to get citations. Also, make sure that there's an image avatar with your company logo. You can update the default image by putting in your logo or put a picture of the team or office.

Here's some visual representation of this. If you log into YouTube and create your channel, you'll get an email confirmation. Once you're set up, you can go to the "My Channel" settings and make some of the updates I referenced on the previous slide.

To change your logo, simply click "change" and choose your image – a very simple step.

Where it says "Your company name," it's going to default to something basic such as your email address on Google. You can hit "change" and update it to say "your city plumbing" or "your city A/C repair services" and then a dash and your company name.

This gives you the chance to get your YouTube channel itself to show up for your keywords in the search engine. You will also have the opportunity to add your channel keywords. That is where you can type in words such as "your city plumber," "your city plumbing," "your city drain cleaning," and of course your company name.

From there, there's a section where you can click "About your company" and put a description about who you are, what you do, and what areas you serve. You can get as creative with this area as you want, but it is most important to make sure you first put a description of your services, and your city.

If you're in Tampa, you put Tampa. If you're in Lakeland, you put Lakeland. If you're in Los Angeles, you put Los Angeles. Put your phone number and, again, restate your name, address and phone number. Citations are important. Having this in the description area is powerful citation source. Always put your name, address and phone number the same way as you did on your Google Map listing, your Angie's List listing, etc. That way, you will be consistent across the web, improving the probability of ranking in the Google Map listings.

Now, let's talk about video tagging best practices. Let's say you created the inventory of videos I recommended: an intro video and clips for each of your services.

How did you tag those videos to maximize the opportunity and to make sure that you're going to rank well in search?

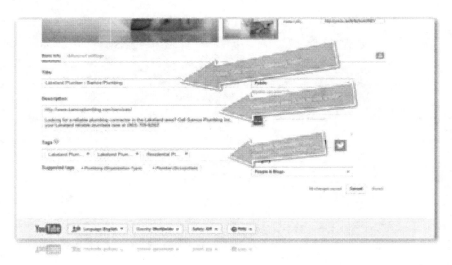

Title Video with City Service - Company (always mix this up a little)

• Description should always start with http://url.com and then describe the service using those same keywords. ALWAYS ADD N.A.P. INFO AT THE

BOTTOM OF THE DESCRIPTION
• Use your keywords as tags and include the company name.
• Choose most appropriate screenshot
• Click "advanced settings" and add address to video

The first thing you want to do is have your primary keywords in the title of the video as well as a description that includes the "http://" before your web address.

In the description area, you can put in "We're a full service XYZ company. We serve this area. This is our name, address and phone number," but at the very top, you should have your website address, including the "http://".

If you just put www.yourcompany.com, YouTube won't understand the link and it will show that it isn't clickable. If you put "http://" the link will be clickable, and visitors will go straight to your page, and they also get the link authority from having that link back to your website.
Choose the screenshot and add video. Whenever you upload your video you are able to to control your title and your description, as well as the ability to add tags.

Again, don't call your videos "your company name." Don't call it "drain cleaning." Don't call it "water heater repair." Call it "Your city + that service," and then your company name. Title your videos the same way that somebody would search.

If it's your intro video, you might want to call it "your city + your primary service" Ex. you're a local "Lakeland plumber   central plumbing." If it's the emergency plumbing page, "your city emergency plumbing services company name".

It is really critical that you have the right titles on your video. It is what is going to make it so that Google can locate it and include it in search results.

The next thing you want to do in your description is to put the link at the very top. The first thing you want to do is include a link back to the home page or to the specific page that you're discussing in the video.

If it's the drain cleaning page, don't put a link to your home page. Put a link to that drain cleaning page, and again "http://yourcompany.com" make sure you've got that "http://".

Below, you add your tags. Within those tags you can put in your city plumber, your city plumbing, your city drain cleaning, and everything in between.

WHAT ELSE CAN YOU DO WITH YOUR VIDEOS?

Now that you've updated your video and you've properly optimized it, your title is correct, and your description is posted, how can we use these videos? Where are we going to leverage them? Well, to really get the benefits of that conversion component, we need those videos to be posted on our website and social profiles as well.

The best way to do this is to copy the "embed code" and post the videos right on your site. The intro video should be embedded on the home page and the service-specific videos should be posted on the appropriate sub-pages. The way we do this is right within our YouTube channel or You-Tube account.

Go to the video manager and find the list of all of the videos that you have. Choose the video that you want to post on your website, and choose the share and embed option.

You will then be provided with this little piece of code, and that's what I have highlighted on the screen. It goes from I frame to I frame. This is the specific code for that video. If you are updating your website on your own, copy and paste the code right into your website's HTML. If you have a detached web manager, send the code off to them with details on where you want it posted.

Once the code is embedded in your HTML, it will show up on the page itself. That's what we really want to do with these videos. And, of course we don't have to limit ourselves to YouTube. There are a lot of very well known video sharing sites out there.

See specific video examples at
www.contractorseo.net/video-marketing

11

LEVERAGE EMAIL MARKETING
TO CONNECT WITH YOUR CUSTOMERS ON A DEEPER LEVEL, GET MORE REVIEWS, GET MORE SOCIAL MEDIA FOLLOWERS AND ULTIMATELY GET MORE REPEAT AND REFERRAL BUSINESS.

Since email communication existed, has been Email Marketing. Email Marketing is one of the oldest forms of advertising your business on the Internet. Although it gets a bad rap because of all the spam going around, it's still one of the most effective forms of marketing.

I am a big believer in email marketing. It's a powerful way to get instant traffic to your website and getting the telephone to ring; but there is a right way and a wrong way to use it.

Did you know the easiest customer to sell to is the customer you already have?

Every self proclaimed marketing expert will tell you that that's noting new. With that said, many business owners hardly ever market or keep in touch with their existing client base. Companies will spend thousands of dollars trying to get new customers but never think to ever into the clients who already buy from them.

Why is that? I have a lot of ideas about this. I suspect business owners think that once a customer buys from them, they will just keep coming back on their own. Or, maybe they simply don't want to bother their customers. The truth is, customers want to hear from you and they want to be touched by your business. If you don't, your competition will.

HOW DO WE START AN EMAIL MARKETING CAMPAIGN?

The first thing you need is an email marketing service. You shouldn't do this yourself for several reasons:

1. Your Internet Service Provider (ISP) will blacklist you for sending bulk mail.
2. You would have no stats for tracking your open emails
3. It would look unprofessional coming from your Microsoft Outlook box

With that said, lets take a look at some of the popular email marketing services, all of which are paid services and are priced based on the amount of emails you send. They all start at around $15.00 per month to send a couple hundred emails.

CONSTANT CONTACT

I have used Constant Contact in the past and I like it for several reasons. It has great tracking stats, the ability to post to your social networks and a pretty user friendly interface.

Constant Contact has many templates available for use. Or, you can add your own custom templates. I think custom templates are a MUST for any business wanting to promote their brand. You will have to know a bit of HTML but if you don't, you can have a web designer create one for you at a fairly inexpensive cost.

MAILCHIMP

Mailchimp is another service I have personally used and recommend. It's fairly easy to use and offers similar features to Constant Contact. The interface is clean and easy to use. Prices start at $10.00.

iCONTACT

Personally, I have never used iContact, but after reading about it on their website www.icontact.com, it looks fairly intuitive and similar to both MailChimp and Constant Contact.

I think all of these services are a good solution for the contractor looking to add email marketing to his or her internet marketing strategy.

HOW TO GET AN EMAIL ADDRESS

I am asked on a regular basis about how to get email addresses. It's really not as easy as sending a letter in the USPS mail to anyone you want to. The reality of it is that just because they are your customer and you have their email address, doesn't mean you can send them anything if you don't have their permission.

This certainly is a fine line, because you somehow already have their email address, and they have used your services before, so is it really considered spam? Technically, yes. You didn't ask them if you could send them specials or a newsletter in email form.

The first thing you really want to do is get your clients' permission to add them to your email list. There are a variety of ways to do this, including placing a form on your website, putting a sign-up sheet on your counter or even a putting a space on your job ticket that they sign when you complete your service.

Explain that you send out tips about your industry or specials on a monthly basis, and would love to have them on your mailing list. You might even offer a discount coupon off your services if they sign up.

Getting that email address is valuable, so if it cost you 5%, go for it. Remember, you want the opportunity to have your company's name in front of your customers every single month. You want to remain top-of-mind if one of their friends are looking for services like yours or if they run into an emergency.

I had a plumber come to my home several years ago. He did a good job and was very professional. Four or five years later, I needed the services of a plumber again. I lost his business card and could not remember the name of his company. I had to find another plumber. He lost the business because he never stayed in contact with me. It was a big job that he lost, $1,500.00 to be exact.

Start building your list today!

WHAT TO SEND AND HOW OFTEN

First, what do I send? You must use the 80/20 rule, 80 percent good information and 20 percent sales. If all you send is emails about what services you offer, no one will ever read it. It's a great way to kill your list.

Draft up some information about your industry, give good homeowner tips, throw in some DIY tips, and make sure it's information that will help your users. For the 20% sales, add a coupon or a special you are having, or offer something for your customers' friends and family.

How often you send your emails is very important. I always go with once per month, around the same time every month. It is important to commit to a date. More than once a month is too much and annoys people. I get an email from a company I purchased from in the past and get 3-4 emails a week from them, 100% sales, sometimes several times a day. I HATE IT and it drives me nuts. I removed myself from that list very quickly as I'm sure others have as well.

GET LEGAL

Make sure you have allow customers the option to Opt Out of receiving email messages at the bottom of every message. Make sure that it's easy because nothing is more annoying than receiving emails that you don't want. If someone does not want to receive your messages, then remove them from your list. They may be getting emails from too many sources and just want to clean out their email box. It does not mean they will never buy from you again. But I will tell you this, if they want out and you keep sending email to them, it's a sure-fire way to bother them and they will likely never buy from you again

Again, you want to leverage email marketing as part of your overall internet marketing strategy. The best way to use it is to be sure you're collecting the email address from all of your customers and prospects. From there, use email marketing to get online reviews, engagement on your social media accounts and remain top-of-mind as a strategy to get more repeat and referral business.

12

OVERVIEW OF PAID ONLINE ADVERTISING OPPORTUNITIES

If we revisit the Online Marketing Plan referenced in chapter one of this book, you will recall that the foundation of your internet marketing plan should be focused on the organic, non-paid marketing efforts (Website, SEO, Google Maps, Social Media Marketing, Video Marketing, etc.), and that once you have a strong foundation, you should have the financial resources to invest in other paid online marketing initiatives.

In this chapter, I want to quickly recap the paid online marketing options that you should consider:

• Pay-Per-Click Marketing on Google AdWords and Microsoft Search (Yahoo & Bing)
• Paid online directory listings on sites like Angie's List, Yelp.com, YP.com
• Pay-Per-Lead and Lead Aggregators like Home Advisor, Contractors.com, Service Magic, etc.

Now, lets talk about the most powerful of these strategies – Pay-Per-Click Marketing.

13

PAY-PER-CLICK MARKETING (GOOGLE ADWORDS AND BING SEARCH) - HOW TO MAXIMIZE THE PROFITABILITY OF YOUR PAY-PER-CLICK MARKETING EFFORTS

In this chapter, we're going to talk about Pay-Per-Click Marketing to help you understand how it works, why it should be integrated into your overall strategy, and how you can run a really effective program that can drive nice, profitable business for you and your company.

WHY PPC SHOULD BE PART OF YOUR OVERALL ONLINE MARKETING STRATEGY

- Start showing up quickly
- Show up as often as possible where your customers are looking
- Show up for non geo-modified terms, such as "plumber", "plumbing", "water heater repair," etc.

First of all, PPC gets things happening quickly, unlike an SEO program, setting up your website, building links and having the right on-page optimization. That process takes a little bit of time to materialize. What you do today and tomorrow, will start to pay dividends in three to four months.

With PPC advertising, you set up your campaign and will start to see your ads serve in just a few days. It can drive good traffic, especially during the times when you need to make sure you're visible.

For example, during the winter season when customers turn their heat on and off on a regular basis, it's a great time to be a heating company because people will likely research that service. We looked at the differences between the paid listings, the organic listings and the map listings.
You want to show up as often as possible when someone's looking for your services. Having a pay-per-click ad that shows up somewhere in the top, on the map, and in the organic section is important. Now you've got

the opportunity to show up multiple places and significantly improve the chances of getting your ad clicked on, as opposed to your competition. A pay-per-click campaign gives you that additional placeholder on the search engines on page one.

It also gives you the opportunity to show up for words that you're not going to show up for in your organic SEO efforts. This is what I like to call non-geo-modified keywords. SEO and our whole organic strategy gives us the ability to show up I search engines when someone types in your city service, your city AC repair, your city roofer, your city pool builder, etc. All of those include some kind of geo-modifier (your city). They're going to put their city or their sub-city in that search for you to rank.

With a pay-per-click campaign, you can show up for the non-geo-modified terms (Ex. roofer, roofing, kitchen remodeler, plumbing service, pool contractor, fence builder, etc.), and put in the settings that you only want to show up for people within a 25-mile radius of your office. If you're in Miami and somebody searches within that area for "plumber" or "plumbing," you can set it so that it only shows your ad for the people that are searching within that area. And Google can manage that through IP addresses by isolating where the search took place.

Google can also isolate who ran that search, where they ran that search from, and then place the ads based on the advertisers that are set up for that area. You only pay on a per-click basis, but you're able to show up for those keywords in those major markets. Another reason that you want to consider running a pay-per-click campaign is because you can run mobile PPC campaigns. With mobile PPC campaigns, when somebody is searching for your services from a mobile device, it's typically because they need immediate service. They're not as apt to browse multiple pages or listings. Now, if somebody runs a search on their mobile device, and you have a pay-per-click campaign set up, that search will be PPC enabled. They can simply hit your ad and, rather than browsing to your website and researching, automatically be calling your company.

On a pay-per-click campaign through mobile, you're actually paying per call as opposed to paying per lead. It's very powerful, and these are the reasons you want to have pay-per-click as part of your overall Internet marketing plan.

THE PAY-PER-CLICK NETWORKS

- www.google.com/Adwords
- bingads.microsoft.com/

So what are the pay-per-click networks? There are two major networks that manage pay-per-click advertising across almost all of the major search engines There's Google AdWords, which is Google's pay-per-click program, and then there is Bing, which is through Microsoft Search.

These both have their own network behind them, so when you pay for an ad or pay-per-click campaign on Google's search network, you're gaining access to AOL, AT&T, USA Today, and Ask.com. When you get on the Microsoft Bing search network, you're getting access to Yahoo!, Facebook, Dogpile, and Excite. There are a variety of reasons to consider a Bing Microsoft pay-per-click strategy.

You can review the chart above to see where most people search and what's going to give you the most attention. It clearly shows that Google is the dominant player with no serious competition. More than 80 percent of all searches happen on Google.com. So, if you had to choose, you would obviously you want to use Google. However, you do get an additional 20 percent by tapping into Bing and Yahoo!. There are different networks but those two make up the majority of the search market. Running a pay-per-click campaign on both Google AdWords and Microsoft Bing search will allow you to show up in the majority of the search engines that somebody might be using.

UNDERSTANDING THE GOOGLE ADWORDS AUCTION PROCESS

Let's review how Google AdWords works. In the simplest sense, you're paying on a per-click basis and you can choose your keywords (Ex. plumber, plumbing, your city plumber, your city emergency plumbing, drain cleaning). As you pick those words, you bid and you pay on a per-click basis.

So, let's just say you're bidding on the keywords "San Antonio Plumber," and there are a lot of other plumbing companies in that city that want to rank for that keyword. If you say that you'll pay $2.00/click and your competitor says that they'll pay $5.00/click, they're going to be at the top.

Assuming nobody else has placed a higher bid, $2.00 is going to be ranked second and $1.20 is going to follow. I am about to explain why that isn't 100% of the reality. The fact is that you pay on per-click basis and you are bidding against the competitors to determine how you're going to rank on your keyword.

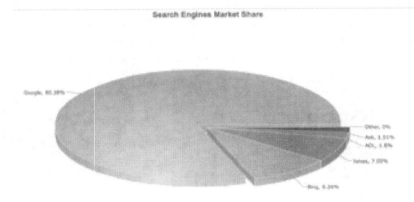

It's an auction, just like eBay. People are bidding and whoever can offer the most money is going to have the strong position. With that foundational understanding, we can now explain why most pay-per-click campaigns fail. What tends to happen is a lot of pay-per-click campaigns are built on the notion that the highest bid wins. So, advertisers pick their keywords, throw up the highest bid per click and hope that everything turns out the way they want it.

WHY MOST PAY-PER-CLICK CAMPAIGNS FAIL

- Setup only ONE ad group for all services (plumbing, emergency plumbing, drain cleaning, water heaters, etc.)
- Don't use specific text ads and landing pages for groups of keywords
- No strong call to action or OFFER on the landing page

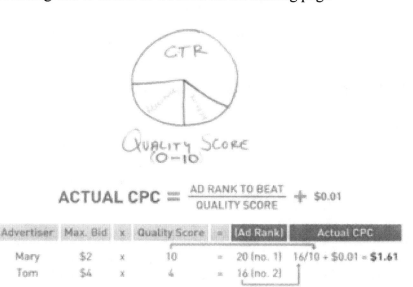

Typically, you setup only one ad group for all services, whether it's plumbing, drain cleaning, emergency plumbing, water jetting, emergencies, etc. You should have one ad group instead of different ad groups for each type of service. Also, there's no specific text ads and no landing pages for those ad groups and groups of keywords.

What you wind up with is the same landing page and the same text ad, whether your customer typed in "plumbing," "emergency plumbing," "water heaters," or "hydrogenic leak detection" in the search engine. Whatever was typed into the search engine was likely very specific, and should match up to a very specific page, but that doesn't happen. It all goes to the home page. With this strategy, not only is your campaign going to convert poorly, but your cost-per-click is going to be higher. I will explain why later in this chapter.

The other reason why most pay-per-click campaigns fail is because there isn't a strong call-to-action on the landing page. So, you were just charged $5.00 or $9.00 to get a potential customer to your website and the page isn't even compelling because it does not have a strong call-to-action. It doesn't tell the consumer what to do next. If you factor these common reasons that pay-per-click campaigns tend to fail, you can better prepare yourself and set yourself up for success in the way that you execute your pay-per-click marketing.

UNDERSTANDING THE ADWORDS AUCTION PROCESS

Let's talk about how the AdWords Auction process actually works. It's not as simple as the highest bidder winning. It's more complicated than that. The reality is, Google needs to feature the most relevant results because their endgame is to get people to keep using their search engine over the competition. This is how they can keep their traffic up.

They can keep their usage up and maintain that 80% market share, but can also run AdWords and make billions of dollars per year. Ultimately it all comes down to relevancy. The second they sacrifice relevancy for dollars, is the second they start to become less of a player in their market. So, they had to figure out a way to make their pay-per-click program grow around relevancy. And so that's why they established the quality score. They need to make sure that the person or company who has more relevancy gets a higher quality score and as result, can have a lower cost-per-click.

The way I like to explain it is, if I go to Google and I type in "BMW," obviously I am looking for a BMW dealer or for information about BMW. Mercedes could say, "That's our demographic also. If someone types in BMW, they're looking for a high-end vehicle. They are probably in the market to buy. Why don't I bid on the word BMW?" Of course they can. However, the person that searched BMW isn't looking for Mercedes. So Mercedes could say, "I"ll pay $25.00 for everybody that clicks on me when they search 'BMW'.

But, BMW might say, "That's my brand and I am going to compete for it, but I am not going to spend $25.00 for every click on my own brand. I'll pay a dollar for every click." Based on quality score, Google may decide to serve BMW because it's in the best interest of the person researching the brand, the consumer. It's also in the best interest of overall relevancy. That's how quality score works. Quality score is really driven by three core components

• Click Through Rate
• Relevance
• Quality of landing page.

As somebody conducts a search and your website shows up on the page in the pay-per-click section, Google is tracking what percentage of those people saw your ad and wound up clicking through. That's one of the primary metrics that they analyze. So, if your ad is relevant, if it speaks to the person's needs, and if it's compelling enough to them that they click through, Google just made more per-click. This will make them willing to give you a higher quality score because you've got better click-through rate.

Also, relevancy is a major factor. How relevant is your text ad to the keyword that was typed?

Example: If they type in "tankless water heaters," and your text ad reads

"We're an emergency plumbing service in the Dallas area,"
vs.
"We specialize in tankless water heaters here in the Dallas area. Click here for immediate water heater repair."

Which do you think is more relevant to the customer? Google wants their search results to be as applicable as possible. They're looking at your click-thru rate, they are looking at the relevancy of your text ad to your keywords, and they are looking at the quality of your landing page.
If your landing page (the page that you drive people to) doesn't match up with what the person just clicked based on your text ad, or if that landing page doesn't have a strong call-to-action and the person quickly returns to the search engine, that signals to Google that you were not very relevant. This will result in a quality score reduction.

Better Quality Score =
Lower Cost Per Click for Top Positions

By having a higher quality score you can bid lower and still achieve the top position. This is where you can actually win in the pay-per-click marketing game because a better quality score results in a lower cost-per-click for those who hold the top positions.

Again, if we just look at the reason most pay-per-click campaigns fail, it's because:

• You only set up one ad group
• You had the opportunity to create a separate ad group for each one of your core services, but you don't use a specific text ad that's going to compel someone to click and improve your click-through rate
• You don't have a strong call-to-action that matches up with what the consumer was looking for
• You're not going to have high click-through rate, relevancy, or an applicable landing page.

All of these issues result in a lower quality score.

You're going to wind up paying more per-click. PPC marketing is very competitive. If you're paying more per-click you're not going to be able to spend that much because you won't be getting enough calls to generate return on investment. The visual representation of this would be like setting up one AdWords campaign for each one of these services (plumbing, emergency, water heater repair, drain cleaning, garbage disposal repair, etc.) and landing people on your home page. That is a recipe for disaster.

That's exactly what you don't want to do.

HOW TO SETUP YOUR PPC CAMPAIGN FOR SUCCESS

Let's talk about how to position your pay-per-click campaign for success. What can you do to ensure the highest probability of success in your pay-per-click campaign? For starters, set up ad groups based on the specific groups of services that you offer (we're going to map this out using a plumbing business as an example). Write compelling text ads that are relevant to your specific keywords or services. Then, link your ads to the specific pages on your site rather than the home page. But, the specific pages on your site that talk about that service should have a strong call-to-action combined with an offer.

What ad groups should you use? What ad groups do you need to set up for your business? Using a plumbing company as an example:

What Ad Groups should you use?

- General Plumbing Services
- Emergency Plumbing
- Water Heater Repair / Replacement
- Drain Cleaning
- Garbage Disposal Repair
- Re-Piping
- Septic Pumping / Cleaning
- Bathroom Remodeling
- Leak Detection
- Trecnhless Sewer Replacement
- Etc, Etc, Etc

If you are in the plumbing business, you need to have standard plumbing for the general, "I need a plumber," or "I'm in need of plumbing services" search. They didn't get very specific. You should have something for that. Have emergency plumbing services available, for the person who types in "emergency plumbing," "emergency plumber," "emergency plumbing services," "24-hour emergency plumber," etc. You want to group those keywords together and have information available for that.

You also want to have one for your water heater repair, water replacement keywords, drain cleaning, garbage disposal repair, re-piping, septic plumbing and cleaning, bathroom remodeling, leak detection, and trenchless sewer replacement. We could go a lot deeper than this, but you should have an idea of what specific types of ad groups you need to set up. From there, you want to write a specific text ad that speaks to that group of keywords.

Then, you will want to drive them to a landing page on your website that has got a compelling call-to-action, that provides what they were looking for and mirrors what your text ad said. I've got a template below to review:

- Pick your list of keywords.
- Write a specific text ad that matches up with what those people are looking for.
- Drive them to a landing page on your website.

Make sure that you've got compelling content on that landing page that emphasizes what they were looking for and prompts them into action, ideally with some type of coupon or special offer, so that they don't keep looking around.

PLUMBING ADWORDS EXAMPLE

Let's look at the plumbing example. Within general plumbing repair, you're going to have the following keywords :

• Plumbing
• Plumber
• Plumbing service
• Plumbing contractor
• Your city plumber
• Your city plumbing
• Plumbing company
• Best plumbers
• Affordable plumbers

These are the keywords that go into this general plumbing ad group. Your text ad should speak to that search.

**"Affordable Dallas plumber, get $50 off,
save, same day service, call now."**

You want to pull on the psychological triggers. Are they looking for affordability? Are they looking for quick service? Typically they are.

Then, drive them to the URL on your site that is specifically targeted at plumbing, Yourcompany.com/Dallas_plumbing_services. Get them to the page that talks about that specific service.

There are a lot of things you can do on the landing page, but you want to make sure that you tap into that psychological trigger.

• Are you looking for quality plumbing services in the Dallas area? Con tact the experts at YourCompany for immediate quality and affordable services at this 555-5555. Then, restate your valuable proposition. There's got to be things that you do that make you different than your competition. Talk about those. Do you have a guarantee? Do you promise to be on time? Do all your guys come in in professional logoed shirts? Do they put booties on their feet?

Talk about why they should choose you and not the competition, and have a link to a page where they can see some external resources. What does the BBB say about you? What reviews do you have on Angie's list? Give them some information so that they can feel confident that you're a credible organization that's going to follow through on your promise. Then, have a strong offer with a call-to-action. Get $50 off your service by referencing the coupon below. Call now! If you have the capabilities built into your website, consider linking them to a form where they can choose to type in their name and phone number and schedule the service right on the spot.

This is a well-crafted ad group specifically for the plumbing keywords.

EMERGENCY PLUMBING

Let's look at emergency situations. The consumer typed in plumbing emer-

INTERNET MARKETING & SEO FOR CONTRACTORS

gency, emergency plumber, 24-hour plumber, 24-hour plumbing service, same day plumbing, after hours plumbing, etc. These are people that are in an immediate need of plumbing services. You want to group those keywords together, save it as an ad group, and create a text ad that is specific to that.

• "Do you have a plumbing emergency in Dallas? Get immediate response and save $50. Call now."

You're say just what they want to hear. They've got an emergency and you're entering the conversation that's already going on in their head. You're offering them some type of incentive to do business with you. Again, you drive them to the emergency plumbing page on your website (ex. www.yourcompany.com/emergenyc-plumbing. Then have some content that speaks to that specific situation.

• "Do you have a plumbing emergency in the Dallas area? When you've got a plumbing emergency, you need somebody that can get out to your home immediately. You can't wait a day. You can't even wait six hours. You want to know that you can get somebody into your home within the hour. Well, at XYZ Plumbing, we specialize in emergency service. We've got a crew standing by. We can have somebody to your house within an hour, guaranteed."

Then, restate that valuable proposition. Show them reviews. Give them an offer, "Get $50 off your next service by referencing the coupon below. Call now."

When you set up your ad groups this way you're going to have high relevancy, you're going to have a higher click-through ratio, and your conversions are going to be better because you're speaking directly to the consumers' needs. You are also giving them some type of call to action and maybe even a special incentive to choose you right at that moment. If you are a remodeler and the person typed in any type of remodeling term, then you need to have a specific AdGroup for that and a slightly different approach.

You can pick bathroom remodeling, bathroom renovation, bathroom contractor, bathroom remodeling contractor, remodel bathroom, etc.
• "Thinking of remodeling your bath in Dallas? Get a free estimate by calling today."

Drive them to the bathroom remodeling page on your website.

On that page, speak to the specific search.

• "Are you thinking of remodeling or renovating your bathroom in the Dallas area? Contact the experts at XYZ Plumbing for quality, afford able bathroom remodeling service." Restate your valuable proposition and show them some pictures of bathroom's you have remodeled before.

In some cases, you will be dealing with services that have a longer purchasing cycle. Air Conditioners, for example. If it's AC replacement or AC installation, if it's bathroom remodeling, or even re-piping, customers are not necessarily going to pick up and call right at that moment. They might just be in the researching process. For these types of services, offer them something for free, such as a buyers guide, design ideas, or 10 things to know before you re-pipe your home. Have a lead capture form, where they can enter their name and their email address to download those guides. This gives you the ability to catch people when they're in the first stages of their evaluation process. Send them a really well-crafted guide that talks about what they should be thinking about and sets the buying criteria in your favor. Why would they want to choose your company versus the competition? What things do they need to be made aware of? Do they need to make sure that they're dealing with somebody that is licensed and insured? Do they need to make sure that they're dealing with somebody that actually understands the design and aesthetics behind a bathroom model, as opposed to just throwing in a toilet and some faucets? In that guide, you can really position yourself and educate them in a way that will make them want to utilize your services.

You can also use email marketing to send them messages over time. If they're at the beginning of a bathroom remodel project, you do your best to catch them early. Maybe it's going to be six months before they decide to make the final decisions or to move forward with any type of project. Because you got their email you could send them one email per week for the next six months. They're going to get something new from you once a week. Nothing annoying, but, "Here's an update, here's another thing, here's another bathroom concept you can look at". When they do get to the point that they are ready to move forward, they've seen you so many times and you've added so much value that they have no choice but to choose your company. You've made the decision easy for them.
This is a way to position yourself better for the longer purchase cycle projects, so you can capture more leads and convert them into customers..

ADWORDS SETUP BEST PRACTICES

Here are some best practices when you get into Google AdWords (google. com/AdWords).

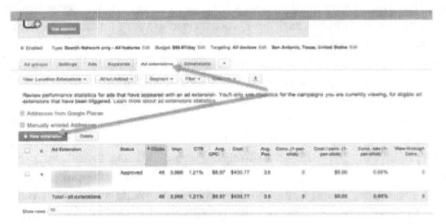

The first one is that you want to make sure you set up an extension with your address. In chapter one, we showed you on how to set up your Google Map listings and optimize it to rank in the Google Map. You want to use the same Gmail account that you claimed your map listing with on

Google AdWords, so that you can come in to extensions and add your address as an extension. This gives you the ability to add your address and a direct link to your Google Places listing in your search.

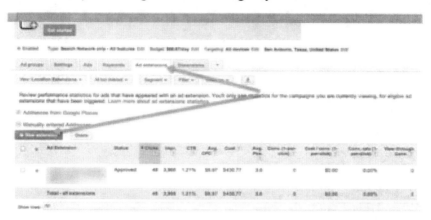

In the screenshot above, you can see this local plumber in Austin, TX listing their website at radiantplumbing.com/austin-tx. Not only do they have their text ad, but they've also got additional real estate on the page with their phone number, a link to their Google Places listing and their address. Can you see how that pops off the page a little more than the others? This is something you definitely want to consider. You want to take the time to set up your AdWords extensions.

HAVE MULTIPLE TEXT ADS FOR EACH ADGROUP AND RUN SPLIT TESTS
The other best practice is to have multiple text ads for every one of your ad groups. This way, you can split test and see each of your ads and determine which one is converting better. Split test by looking at your two ads for emergency plumbing. They're just different variations of the same messaging. They're going to get equal share. If there are one thousand impressions, you could distribute 500 to one, and 500 to the other.
By split testing, you will be able to determine which one had a higher click-through rate. With that information, you can drop out the lower performing ad and create a new one. Then at the end of the month, you can compare those two ads and see which one performed better. You keep doing that so you can continually improve your click-through ratios.

AdWords Best Practices
Have Multiple Versions of your Ads and Split Test for best CTR

Remember, having better click-through rates is going to get you more traffic, but it's also going to give you a better quality score. This will eventually make your cost-per-click lower, making it more profitable for you in the long-term.

PAY ATTENTION TO AVERAGE POSITION

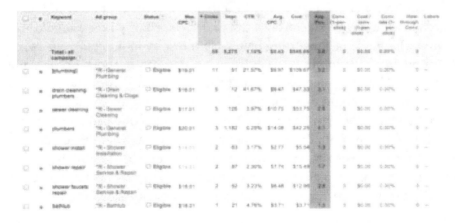

The other thing you want to do is to pay attention to your average position in your Google AdWords campaign. These settings are available making it very easy to analyze the data. In the report above, you can see what position is being maintained. The average position is highlighted. Position 3.6. Then, one is in 3.2, one is in 2.8, and one is in 1.7. This is based on the quality score and the average cost per click. You want to maintain a top four position on the major search engines in your pay-per-click marketing campaign.

We have found that the further down the list they go, the higher probability that you will be attracting a price shopper that's literally clicking every single company along the way.

You don't necessarily need to be the top listing, because that could just be a result of some random person that didn't think through what they're doing. However, you want to maintain a top four position. That's going to give you the best overall visibility, and ultimately, the best return on your investment.

Pay attention to your average cost-per-click, and manage your bids so you maintain a top four position.

EXACT MATCH VS. BROAD MATCH

AdWords Best Practices

• Pay Attention to Exact Match vs. Broad Match
• Add Negative Keywords where appropriate to protect your budget
  ★ Jobs, Employment, Marketing, etc

The other thing you want to pay attention to is exact match versus broad match. You have a setting inside your AdWords campaign where you specify whether you want Exact Match or Broad Match. Always elect to do exact match. The reason is because if you choose broad match, you could very easily find yourself accidentally showing up on the search engines for a lot of keywords that have nothing to do with your specific business. The other thing you want to do is pay attention to negative keywords – keywords that you don't want show up for in the search engine. A great example of this is, jobs, employment, marketing, etc. If someone types in "your city plumber," that's great. If they type in "your city plumbing jobs," that's somebody looking for employment in plumbing. Unless you are trying to fill a positiong or if you actually want to use your pay-per-click budget to get applicants, it's probably not the kind of the person you want to attract.

Setting up negative keywords means, for example, if someone types in "jobs," "employment," or "marketing services" anywhere in their search, it pulls you out of that search. It pulls you out of that specific bidding process so you won't be paying for clicks from somebody that's not relevant to you.

I talked a little bit about making sure that you've set up mobile pay-per-click campaigns. I've mentioned the major transition of people searching on their mobile device versus people searching on their computer.

Mobile PPC

More and more people are accessing the Internet via smart devices; their iPhone, Android, and tablets. The searcher is typically in a different mind-frame when they are searching from a phone rather than from the computer. When you're searching from a phone, you often just want to get the information right away, and/or want your problem solved as soon as possible. You can set up a campaign to have click-to-call built into your mobile campaign. In the image above there was a search conducted from a mobile device, "Dallas Plumber".

Do you see the "Call" button towards the bottom? That's what we call a mobile PPC campaign with the click-to-call function turned on. If somebody hits that "Call" button, they're actually connected immediately to that Benjamin Franklin location. This is a quick alternative to having to search for the website and the phone number on your own. Plus, you can see on a mobile phone there is not a lot of screen space. Those pay-per-click listings become really prominent and they dominate the search results page on mobile. A lot of times, you're going to get the majority of the clicks if you're in those top two positions. It's all about convenience, and the click-to-call function allows that.

It's extremely powerful to connect with these people that are searching from mobile devices. Set up a mobile-specific campaign and choose "Mobile Devices Only." Then you can pick your geolocation. That would be your 30-mile range or 20-mile radius. You then click a button to turn on the click-to-call function. That's how you wind up with a pay-per-click campaign that has you in the top positions if bidded on correctly, with the options for them to do a click-to-call.

Just to recap, you want to set up your ad groups correctly. Make sure that you pick keywords that group them together, you write text ads that speak directly to that group of keywords, and ensure your landing page (where you are sending those specific searches) speaks to the text ads and the group of keywords. You also want to be sure that you have some type of strong call-to-action that prompts your consumer into calling you as opposed to pressing the "Back" button and looking at four or five other competitors. As the relevancy of your ad groups campaign and your keywords improve, your cost-per-click will decline and your conversion will improve. You can spend less and still get better positioning and more traffic to your website. This is how you maximize the profitability of your pay-per-click marketing campaigns and succeed in PPC where others fail.

**To watch a training video on how to implement these concept
& PPC Marketing go to www.contractorseo.net/ppc**

14

PAID ONLINE DIRECTORIES - WHAT PAID ONLINE DIRECTORIES SHOULD YOU CONSIDER ADVERTISING IN (ANGIE'S LIST, YP.COM, YELP.COM, JUDIES BOOK, MERCHANT CIRCLE, ETC.)

In this chapter, we're going to be covering paid online directory listings. We talked about the overall internet market strategy, beginning with the foundation of having a properly optimized website. We have also discussed making sure that you've got yourself set up with all the right pages on your website, the conversion elements, doing the off page optimization for building inbound links, building authority for your domain, having the review acquisition strategy, and making sure that you're ranking in the organic, non-pay-per-click listings for your most important keywords. We then talked about looking at social media and email marketing as a way to connect with your customer on a deeper level, and get more repeated referral business. As you get those non-paid elements of your internet marketing strategy squared away, you can start looking at paid online marketing programs.

We talked about pay-per-click marketing, and the way you could set up an effective pay-per-click marketing campaign on AdWords or Microsoft Bing search in order to show up in the paid listings. In this chapter, I want to talk about other paid marketing components, such as online directory listings that you can pay for to get premium listings.

There's literally hundreds of online directories, from Judy's Book and Angie's list, to City Search, and YP.com, as well as an array of other little secondary directories. I'm going to talk about the ones that are the biggest;

the ones that will help you gain exposure where your customers are looking most.

WHAT ARE THE PAID ONLINE DIRECTORY LISTINGS AND ONLINE SITES THAT YOU SHOULD CONSIDER?

As mentioned, there are literally hundreds of online directory listings. The ones that we have found to be the most prominent and visited are:

• Angie's List
• BBB
• YP.com
• Yelp
• CitySearch and/or CityGrid.

If you have an unlimited budget and you are already doing well with your organics, and you wanted to pay for some additional premium placement in online directories, these are the ones I would suggest that you take into consideration.

YP.com

 The online yellow pages vary area by area. In some markets, its YP.com and in others, it is DexKnows.com, Version Yellow Pages, YellowBook.com or some facsimile there of.

With YP.com and other online yellow pages, you need to be very careful as you get started. You don't want to be roped in to their print Yellow Page ad. The cost goes from a couple hundred bucks a month to potentially a couple thousand dollars per month when you start to get into their Yellow Pages book and their pay-per-click advertising.

Do not let Yellow Pages manage your pay-per-click advertising under any circumstances. There is a whole chapter on Pay-Per-Click Marketing in

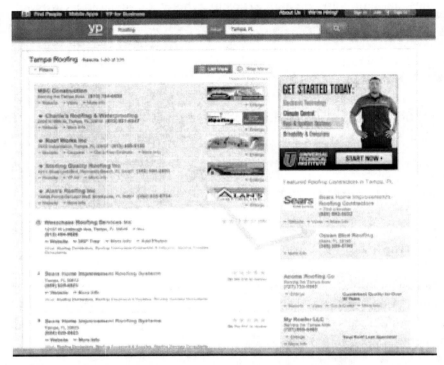

this book. I go in-depth about how to set up an effective pay per click campaign. You don't want to let any of these companies try and touch your pay per click advertising on Google, Yahoo or Bing. Do it the right way. Set up the ad groups on your own.

When I say YP.com, I am really talking about their YP.com website. In your city, there are little boxes and banners that show up at the top and along the side. It maybe worth spending $300.00 to $500.00 per month to show up in that area because there are still plenty of people who visit YP.com when they need your services.

Pay close attention to your tracking to see how many visitors are coming to your website from theirs. Field your calls to find out if they are coming in from it so that you can gauge whether there's true term investment associated with that listing.

CITY SEARCH & YELP

The other two that are lower level are CitySearch and Yelp.com. These are more restaurant related sites. Not as many people go there when they need home service type solutions, but there are still plenty of eyes on their websites overall. If, for some reason, you have a lot of reviews on Yelp. com, it might not be a bad idea to pay for a premium ad on their directory for your services.

BETTER BUSINESS BUREAU

 BBB, the Better Business Bureau is not just an online directory, it is a major sign of credibility. It's not as popular as it once was, but posting the BBB logo and being able to say that you're A+ credited is worth the investment. I haven't found that it allows for a ton of leads, but it's a great credibility symbol and a good thing to be able to reference.

ANGIE'S LIST

Angie's list

I have saved what I feel is the best for the last, when it comes to paid online directory services for your plumbing and HVAC business, and that is Angie's list. From my experience with working with some of largest home services businesses across the country and interviewing multimillion dollar business owners, Angie's list is the go-to place for getting quality inbound calls and customers.

One of the things I like about Angie's list is that you're able to attract the higher quality customers. The customer that are not looking for the low price, but for quality and convenience. In chapter two we looked at marketing fundamentals and talked about knowing what your target market is, knowing who you are selling to and crafting messages that resonate deeply within those specific consumers.

If you determine that you want homeowners, people that are above the age of 35, aren't finicky about price and are willing to pay a premium for quality, professionalism, and timeliness, then Angie's list is going to be your place to reach that target market.

Angie's list customers have paid in order to gain access to a list of quality/ prequalified contractors. Just by that virtue alone, you know that you're going to be dealing with the higher level individual.

Depending upon your market, I would do some research to find out how popular Angie's list is in your area. How many users there in your market? If it's got a lot of users, like in areas such as California, Indianapolis, and Florida, then you definitely want to look into it.

If you are reading this book in Canada, the big website there is Home Stars. That's not one I'm going to talk about here, but if you're in Canada, you definitely want to be on Home Stars to look at a paid placement there. There are a couple of caveats with Angie's list in order to make the paid promotional section of it work. As you look at moving from a free listing to a paid listing on Angie's list, you need to have a lot of good, solid reviews. The foundation that makes your Angie's list profile drive calls and customers is reviews.

You need to have a base of reviews to be successful. If you've already got a handful of good reviews on Angie's list, you are off to a good start. If you don't have any or if you've got a handful of bad reviews, you may wind up struggling and might want to consider passing on the Angie's list altogether. This is because the person searching around for your services is looking to deal with the company that has great reputation and good reviews from other Angie's list users.

With that said, if you don't have a lot of reviews, you will want to leverage the review development process within Angie's list to accelerate your return on investment. As part of your paid advertising program on Angie's List, you are provided with tools that will help you get reviews from your customers.

You can export a database of your customers' names, addresses and email addresses, and they'll bounce that against the Angie's list user database and send an email on your behalf saying, "This company is an active Angie's list member and you did business with them recently. We'd love it if you would write them a review." This can really accelerate the process, helping you to get reviews on Angie's list.

Once you are a member of Angie's list, one of the benefits is that you get badges that you can put on your website. Like the credibility badge provided to you by the Better Business Bureau, you will receive super service awards from Angie's List as you receive positive reviews. You can take these badges and put them on your website and your marketing materials. It's a great credibility symbol coupled with or without the BBB listing.

Here's an example of a site that is really leveraging their Angie's list badges. They won 2012, 2011, 2010, and 2009. The badges are featured above the fold on their website, and customers like to see that. Even if your potential customer is not an Angie's list member, they often know

what Angie's list is. It will even help with conversion from non-Angie's List members.

There are many online directory sites and new services come onto the market every day. This is just my list of the paid directory services that I've personally seen drive a strong return on investment for other home service businesses.

PAY-PER-LEAD AND LEAD SERVICES - HOW TO PROPERLY MANAGE PAY-PER-LEAD SERVICES FOR MAXIMUM RETURN AND LONG-TERM GAINS

Now let's talk about Pay Per Lead services. With these services, you can pay per lead or you can pay on a per-monthly basis to gain access to all the leads that come in in your market. I am not 100% saying you should do this; I am simply suggesting that if you need some additional leads or you've got an inside sales team that can follow up with these proactively, these are some good options.

- HomeAdvisor (Formerly Service Magic)
- eLocal
- ConstructionDeal
- Networx

There are an abundance of these types of services. The best way to find additional lead services specific to your business would be to run a Google Search for "Your Service Lead Service", "Your Service Pay-Per-Lead", etc.

HOW DO PAY PER LEAD SERVICES WORK?

The nice thing about this type of service is that you only pay when you get a qualified lead. With others, you just have a budget. You set $500.00/month to get all of the leads that come in from that area. That's how Networx & eLocal work. With Home Advisor (the biggest player in this space), you pay on a per-lead basis.

If you have followed the plan outlined in this book, you should have your organic keywords ranking well in the search engines and map listings, pro-active social media and email marketing as well as a well structured pay per click marketing campaign. If you want to bump the lead flow, these services can help to start channeling new people that are in the market for your services.

However, you have to be diligent and quick with your follow up. You will hear a lot of horror stories about how badly these lead services work and how you can throw so much money away. I will be the first to say that I don't think it's the place to start. If you have built your internet marketing strategy on pay per lead services, you're destined to fail. You can't build a sustainable business around just this one strategy.

But, if it's an add on to a strong internet marketing program, then it can be relatively effective. The key is to remember that these requests for leads aren't coming to you directly. They're on Home Advisor. They're on e local Plumber. They are sending in an anonymous request for a quote, providing their name and email address knowing that they are going to get phone calls. However, they are probably going to be price conscious shoppers. They are using these services because they want to get the lowest price possible. Keep that in mind.

If you don't have the time and energy to chase leads, then I would say to pass on pay per lead services altogether. These leads also go out to you and a number of other companies in your area, so you have to be aggressive. You have to be the first person to get customers on the phone and you have to be professional with a compelling offer that makes them want to choose you as opposed to the competition.

You also need to setup a follow up system to make sure that you have a fallback plan in place for leads that you can't reach right away. You can get these leads in a variety of formats. They'll send you an email, you can log in and download an Excel list, or you can receive a text message that alerts you as soon as the email comes through.

If you have a dispatcher on your team, be sure to assign somebody specifically to follow up on leads. Know who is accountable for these leads when they come in. If it's going to you, to your dispatcher, or even one of your sales guys, you don't want there to be any confusion about who is responsible for following up because then the lead falls through the cracks.

Specifically assign someone the responsibility of reaching out to these people. Have a predefined script on how the call should be handled. Be professional. Be courteous. Be quick.

A lot of these are going to go to the first person that gets them on the phone, so it is important to be really aggressive. Don't just call once; have a process in place where you reach out to these people 3 to 5 times over the course of the next 24 hours because they're in the window to buy. Then, have a fall back strategy, in the event that you don't get them on the phone. If you don't get them on the line, make sure that you're taking not of their name and their email address so that you can remain top-of-mind with them. The reality is, this is somebody in your service area that is in need of your specialty, so they're probably a home owner.

If you're not sending an email follow-up, and if you're not adding them to your email marketing database, then you're wasting marketing dollars. If you've just spent $5, $10, $25 for that lead and you're not proactively and diligently following up with them via email, you might as well not even pay.

Below is a script of a solid fall back strategy. Set up an email auto-responder on a program such as Aweber or Instant Customer, where your dispatcher can enter the customer's name and email address, and have a series of emails that go out to the customer over the next several days. Remember not to let this be your crutch. Don't think that these emails are going to do the trick.

Email 1 - Subject - Your Recent XYZ Service Inquiry

Customer Name, You recently submitted a request on [LEAD Site] for help with XYZ Services. I called and left a message for you on the number that was listed and look forward to talking with you soon. You can reach me directly at xxx-xxx-xxxx. With so many XYZ companies to choose from in the [YOUR CITY], I know it can be hard to know who you can trust. At XYZ Company we have been serving the [your city] area since 1982 and are dedicated to resolving your XYZ issue quickly, cost effectively and without leaving a mess. Give me a call at xxx-xxx-xxxx to schedule your service.

Email 2 - Special Offer for XYZ Services

Customer Name, You indicated that you were in some need of some XYZ services a few days ago. I'm sure you have received a number of calls from XYZ Company, who are eager to earn your business. WELL – as our outside-of-the-box approach to getting your attention, we want to offer you a special offer. If you call us today and reference this coupon, we will knock 10% off your estimate for services.

<ATTACH COUPON IMAGE>

Call now and get 10% off your plumbing services with XYZ Company.

Email 3 – Subject – RE: Your Recent Plumbing Inquiry

Customer Name, I hope this note reaches you well. You reached out to us earlier this week via [lead site] looking for some help with your XYZ service. We would love to be of service to you. I have tried you a few times on the phone number you listed with no success and don't know if you are just busy or if you already hired another company. Please shoot me a quick reply to let me know if we can be of assistance, or give me a call at xxx-xxx-xxxx

The aggressive follow up work on the phone is what's going to get you the business. But, just have this as a fall back strategy.

Again, don't stop there. You've got their name and email address. You should be marketing to these people via email on at least a monthly basis. You should have an email database of customers and prospects that you should be sending out emails to once a month with some type of update. "Here's what's going on with our company. Here's why you should consider tank less water heaters. Some special offer incentive." This is to remain top-of-mind so that you can build your customer-base both in email and social media.

As you look at paid online advertising and paid-per-lead services, be cautious. Don't overspend. Put the tracking in place to make sure you've got a strong return on investment. If you are going to play the paper lead service game, make sure that you have a proactive, diligent process that touches these people multiple times, via phone and email.

15

TRACK, MEASURE AND QUANTIFY - HOW TO TRACK YOUR ON-LINE MARKETING PLAN TO ENSURE THAT YOUR INVESTMENT IS GENERATING A STRONG RETURN ON INVESTMENT

Now that you've built and optimized your website, you've got an ongoing link building strategy in place where you're creating inbound links and moving up in the search engines, you have implemented email marketing and social media marketing initiatives, and have possibly implemented a paid online marketing campaign including Pay-Per-Click and Pay-Per-Lead services, you need to put some tools in place so that you can track, measure and quantify your data to ensure that you're moving in a positive direction.

There are a lot of different tracking mechanisms that you can put in place. I'm going to recommend three core tracking mechanisms. The first is Google Analytics. Google Analytics is a great website data analysis tool and it's completely free. Google Analytics will show you specifically:

• How many visitors got to your website on a daily, weekly, monthly, and annual basis.
• What key words they typed in to get there.
• What pages on your website they visited.
• How long they stayed.

The main thing you want to see from Google Analytics: when I started this whole Internet Marketing process, how many visitors was I getting to my website? Maybe it was 5, 20, 100, or 500, but it's good to know. Then you can compare to future data on an ongoing basis.

- Google Analytics
  www.google.com/analytics
- Keyword Tracking Report
  www.gshiftlabs.com
- Call Tracking Report -
  www.callfire.com

Ultimately, what you are looking for is whether or not the number of visitors to your website is increasing. Is the variety of keywords that they're finding you with increasing? Are you moving in a positive direction?

You can also set up reports within Google Analytics. To get set up on Google Analytics, you just go to Google.com/analytics. It's a simple process. You verify that you own the website through a variety of different methods, and then you install a small piece of code into your website's HTML. After you have done that, you've got the tracking in place and you're ready to go.

KEYWORD TRACKING

The other tracking mechanism that I recommend is keyword tracking. At the beginning of this process, we talked about keyword research to determine what keywords people are typing in when they need your services. We came up with a list and all of those keywords were combined with your cities and sub cities.

There are tools that will tell you how you're ranking on Google, Yahoo, and Bing for those various keywords. A few options include:

- Bright Local
- White Spark
- Raven Tools
- WebCEO

The keyword tracking tool I recommend is called BrightLocal. You can learn more about it at www.brightlocal.com. There is a cost associated with this service, but it is great resource for tracking your search engine optimization progress. You take your keywords, put them into he Bright-Local Keyword Tracker and then set up a weekly and monthly report that shows where you rank on Google, Yahoo and Bing for your most import-ant keywords.

With a report like this, you can easily see how your website is trending in the search engines.

If you've built out the website correctly with the right on-page factors (title tags, H1 tags, meta descriptions, etc.), if you're building links, developing citations and have a proactive review acquisition system in place, you'll see yourself move up in the results. When you see yourself stagnating, you can go back to that keyword, figure out which page is optimized for it, look at your links and link profile, and whatever is necessary to push that keyword to the next level.

CALL TRACKING

The third really important tracking mechanism that I recommend is call tracking. Having better rankings and more visits to you website is all fine and dandy, but in the home services business, nothing happens until a call is made. Calls are what drives service revenue. You want to have some type of tracking mechanism in place to know how many calls are coming in on a monthly basis and what's happening within those conversations. Are they turning into sales? That's where the rubber meets the road. That's why we're doing all of this. Who cares if you're in the number one position if it doesn't result in dollars to the business? There are a number of call tracking tools that you can use.

- Call Fire
- IfByPhone
- Call Source
- Centry Interactive

One of the tools I've seen used prevalently is called CallFire. You can learn more about it at www.CallFire.com.

Most of these call tracking services will let you choose a phone number based on your area code. So, you type in the number you want to get. It's a nominal fee on a monthly basis ($2 - $5 per month), and you get a tracking number.

Then, you can take that tracking phone number and you can put it on the graphics on your website so that you can track the number of calls and even listen to recordings of the conversation. That number will be set to ring in your office. It's just a forwarding number. If somebody dials it, it still rings to your office like always, but is still a tracking number. You can report on the number of calls using the internet and play back recordings of those conversations. It's extremely powerful to know the number of calls you were getting when you started versus the number after you incorporated your new marketing strategy. You can go in and listen to those conversations and ascertain how many of those calls turned into booked service while knowing what the revenue associated with that service is. That is how you get a true gauge on the return on investment associated with your online marketing strategy.

These are the types of tracking mechanisms I recommend. There are a lot of different things you can do, but having analytics, keyword tracking, and call tracking really gives you the most important key performance indicators to gauge your progress.

16

THE NEXT STEPS

WHAT'S NEXT?

Throughout the course of this book, we have covered an abundance of information. We've mapped out your internet marketing plan and taken you step-by-step through how to claim and optimize your Google map listing, how to optimize your website for the most commonly searched keywords in your area and how to leverage social media to get more repeat and referral business. We then covered paid online marketing strategies like pay-per-click and pay-per-lead services. If you have taken action and followed our instructions, you should be well on your way to dominating the search engines for the keywords in your area.

As a buyer of this book you have access to a training video & implementation guide. To access that training video just go to http://www.contractorseo.net/free

Go to www.contractorseo.net/free

NEED MORE HELP?

If you've gotten to this point and feel like you need some extra help to implement these ideas, we are here to support you. As experts in helping contractors and home services companies across the nation, we have had tremendous success implementing these strategies. You can call us directly at **866-493-9910** with any questions that you might have. Our team will review your entire online marketing effort (Website, Competition, Search Engine Placement, Social Media, etc.) and come back to you with a complete assessment of how you can improve and what you can do to take your online marketing efforts to the next level.

REQUEST A FREE CUSTOM ONLINE MARKETING EVALUATION NOW. YOUR CUSTOM TAILORED OPTIMIZATION AUDIT WILL:

- Identify key issues that could be harming your website without you even knowing it.
- Look at where your website stands compared to your competitors.
- Determine whether SEO is the appropriate route for you to take.
- Uncover hidden revenue that you're leaving on the table.
- Offer recommendations that you can put to use immediately. Josh Nelson

17

ABOUT THE AUTHORS

JOSH NELSON

Josh Nelson is an entrepreneur, author, speaker and internet marketing consultant. He is the CEO of Clic Inc. and heads our primary divisions: ContractorSEO, PlumberSEO, HVACSEO & Roofer SEO. He has a passion for helping companies leverage best practices to increase sales, drive new streams of revenue and accomplish their goals. He's been involved in Web and Internet Marketing for over 12 years and started his own Web Design and Hosting Company in 1999. Over the years, he has worked with hundreds of small and medium-sized businesses and developed strategies to help them grow their business by effectively marketing online via Search Engine Marketing (PPC), Search Engine Optimization (SEO), Social Media (Facebook, Twitter, LinkedIn) and other internet platforms.

You can learn more about Josh Nelson at www.joshnelsonblog.com and his services at www.contractorseo.net.

DEAN IODICE

Dean Iodice has been involved with the Internet since the early days of the dot com industry. "I started in this industry as a Graphic Designer, designing all types of print media. In the early 90's when the dot com era was in high swing I transitioned over to webpage design. I knew the Internet was that **one big thing** of my lifetime and I was going to do everything in my power to be a part of it."

Dean later closed his graphic design business and went to work with ReachLocal the largest PPC marketing company in the United States. It was with ReachLocal I learned a lot about marketing for small businesses.

My time there was short but good in a sence that it has paved the way for a great future. Josh and I met at ReachLocal and made the decision to start our own SEO company. We wanted a business model that worked well and was affordable enough to give ROI for small business owners.

Knowing the importance of specializing in a niche we targeted contractors. Contractors like plumbers, HVAC, Roofers and the like are a natural progression from the Yellow Pages to Internet Marketing.

Together we have grown our company from just the two of us working out of our homes to a team of 13 people. We are not a huge company but we are a special company. Special in the sence that we put the customer first, yeah everyone says that but we live it and preach it. It's all about doing your best so your clients can rank and get results.

FREE BONUS
TRAINING VIDEO & GUIDE

As a buyer of this book you have access to a training video & implementation guide. The video training and guide define your online marketing plan (Website, SEO, Social Media Marketing, PPC, Pay-Per-Lead services, etc.) and walk you step-by-step through the process of rolling out an effective online marking effort for maximum effect in terms of leads, calls, revenue and growth.

TO ACCESS THAT TRAINING VIDEO JUST GO TO
HTTP://WWW.CONTRACTORSEO.NET/FREE

CPSIA information can be obtained at www.ICGtesting.com
Printed in the USA
LVOW06s0340210715

447004LV00026B/543/P